David Kalama's

Photographic Safari
in East Africa

Kenya and Tanzania
in Black and White

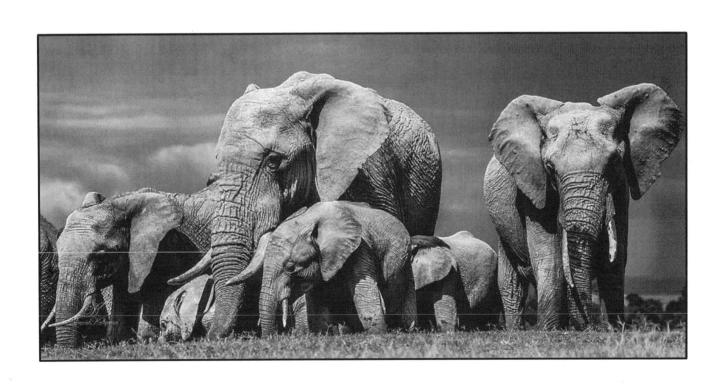

Published in 2018
Kalama Photographic Safaris
info@kalama.co.ke
www.kalama.co.ke

Book design by Barbara Foster

ISBN-13: 978-1983561467
ISBN-10: 1983561460

Camera Equipment
  Nikon D750
  Nikon DX 10-24 mm f/1.8

TAMRON

  Tamron 70-200 mm f/2.8
  Tamron 150-600 f/5-6.3 G2

Dedicated
to my sons

Tristan Israel

TylerDavid

I love photography because it has no limit to what I can do. For the fun of it, I found myself trying black and white photography.

I love to educate and inspire everyone I come into contact with online and on safari. Dear readers, "When you get up every morning, make everything beautiful and colorful. Even when it all seems black and white, let those colors reflect out of you from within. . . a positive attitude. Have faith and believe that anything is possible. You can make ugly beautiful; it all depends on you. You have the power within and without!! Do it!!"

David Kalama Mwadime
Executive Director
Kalama Photographic Safaris

David Kalama's Photographic Safari in East Africa: Kenya and Tanzania in Black and White contains over 100 black and white photographs, some with David's inspirational and educational comments. Enjoy the beautiful people and wildlife photographs taken in the following wildlife areas of East Africa.

Kenya
- Amboseli National Park
- Masai Mara National Reserve
- Nairobi National Park
- Sweetwaters Tented Camp

Tanzania
- Lake Manyara National Park
- Ngorongoro Conservation Crater
- Serengeti National Park

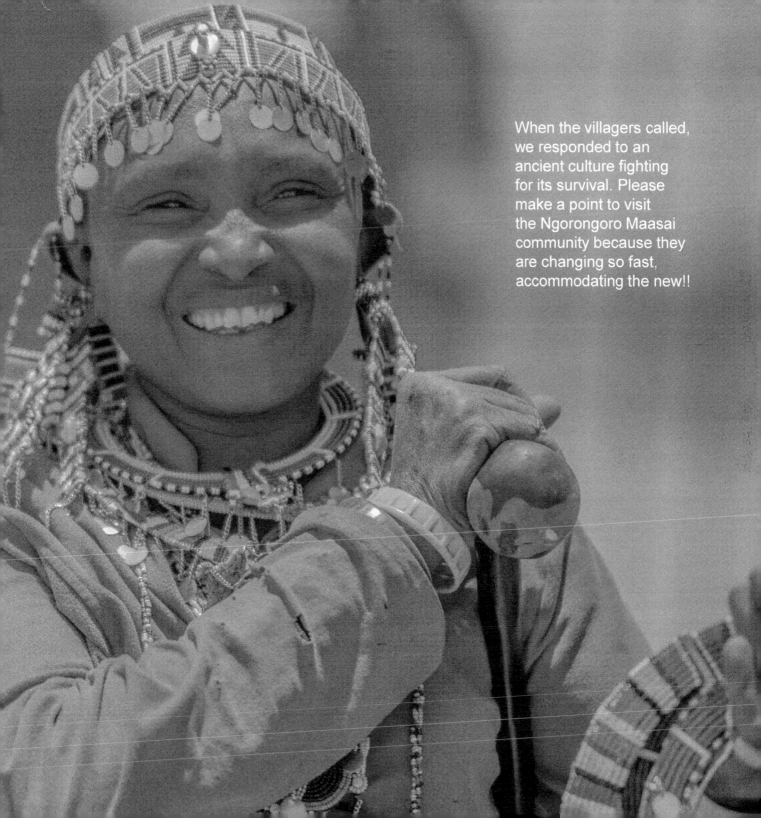

When the villagers called, we responded to an ancient culture fighting for its survival. Please make a point to visit the Ngorongoro Maasai community because they are changing so fast, accommodating the new!!

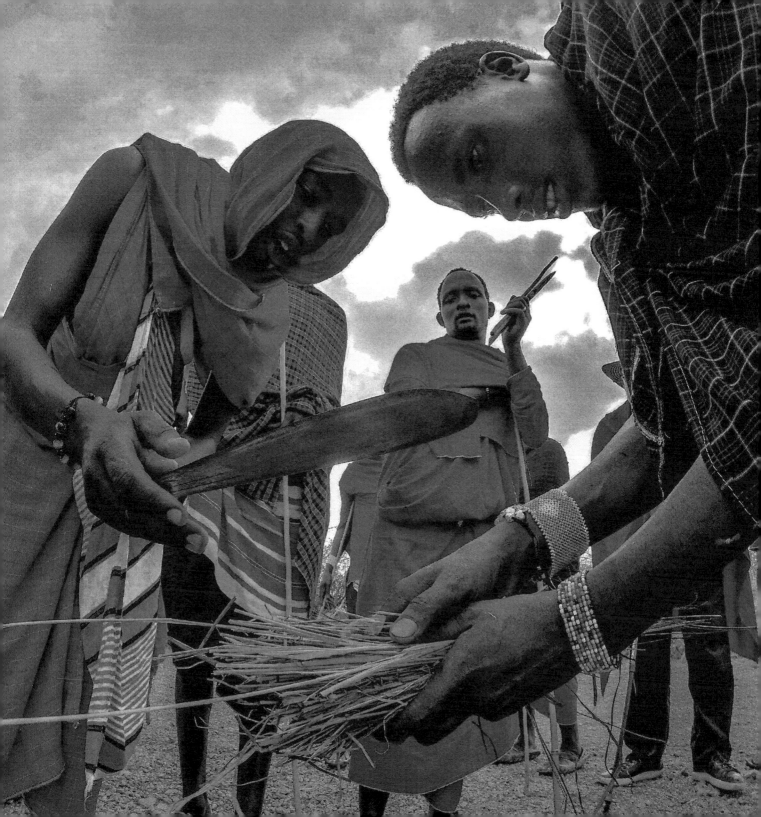

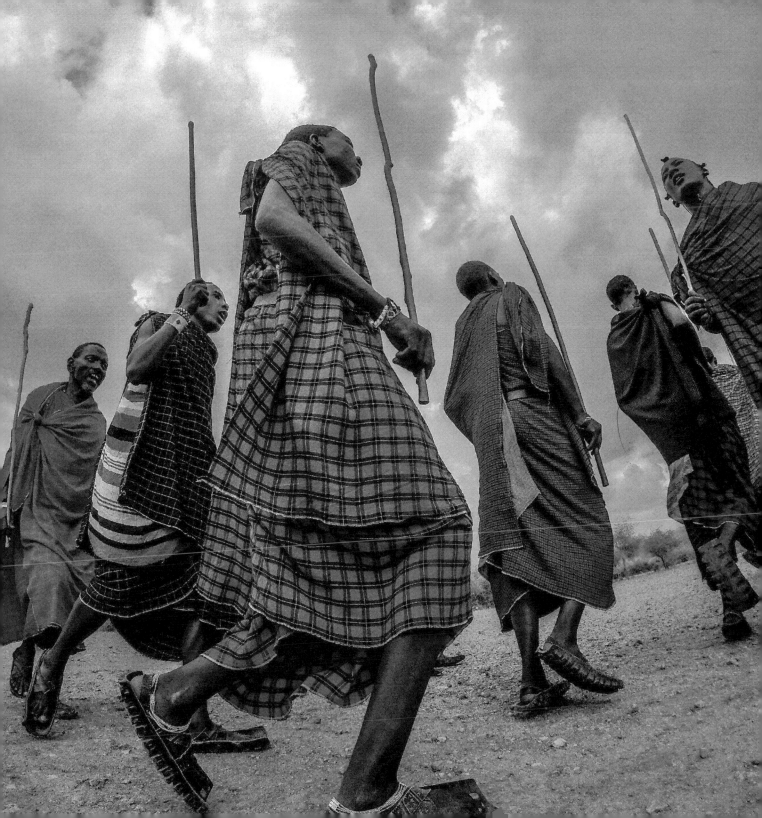

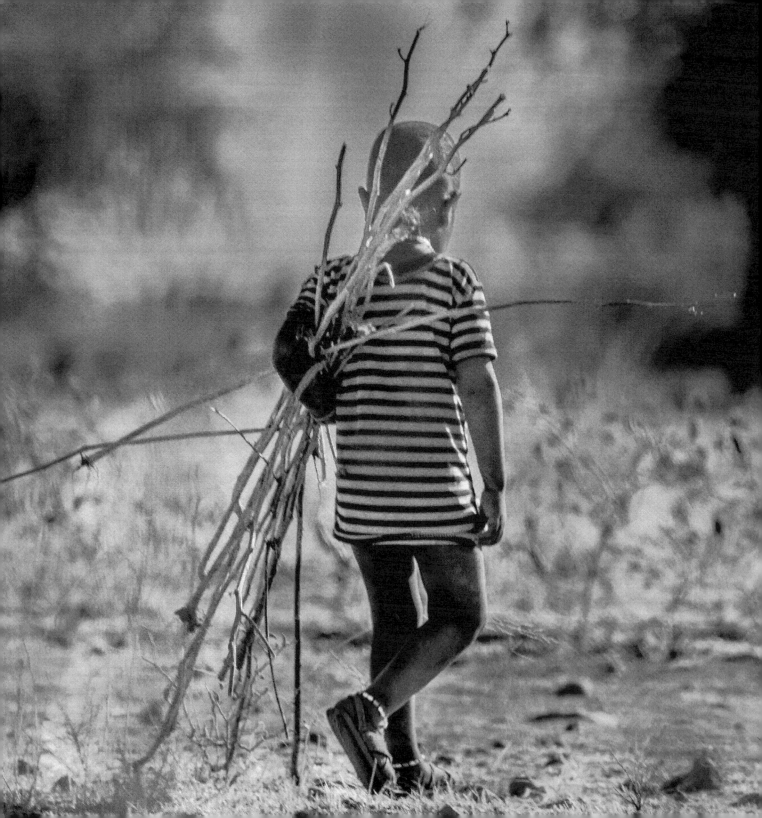

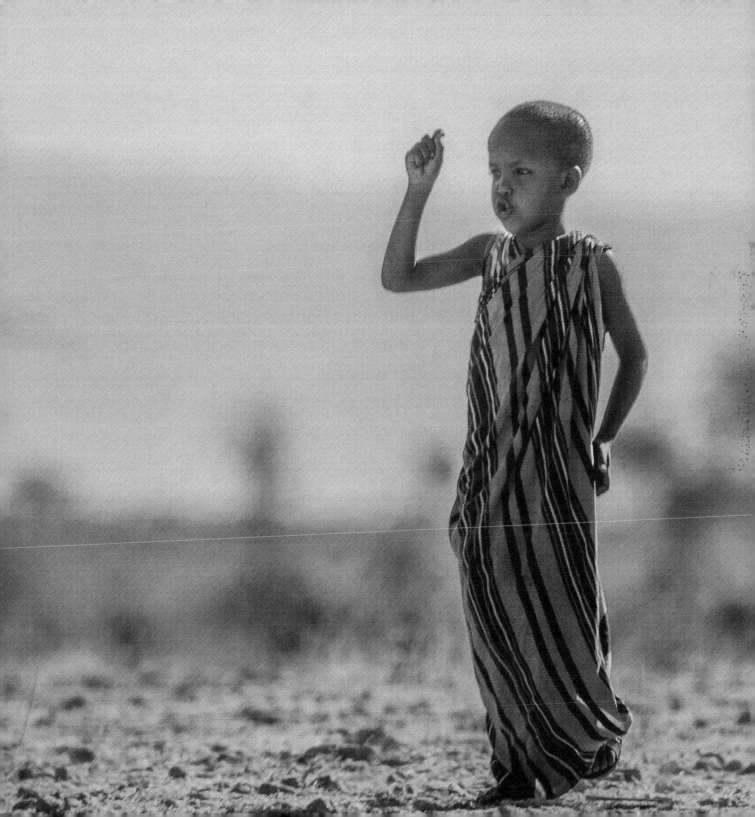

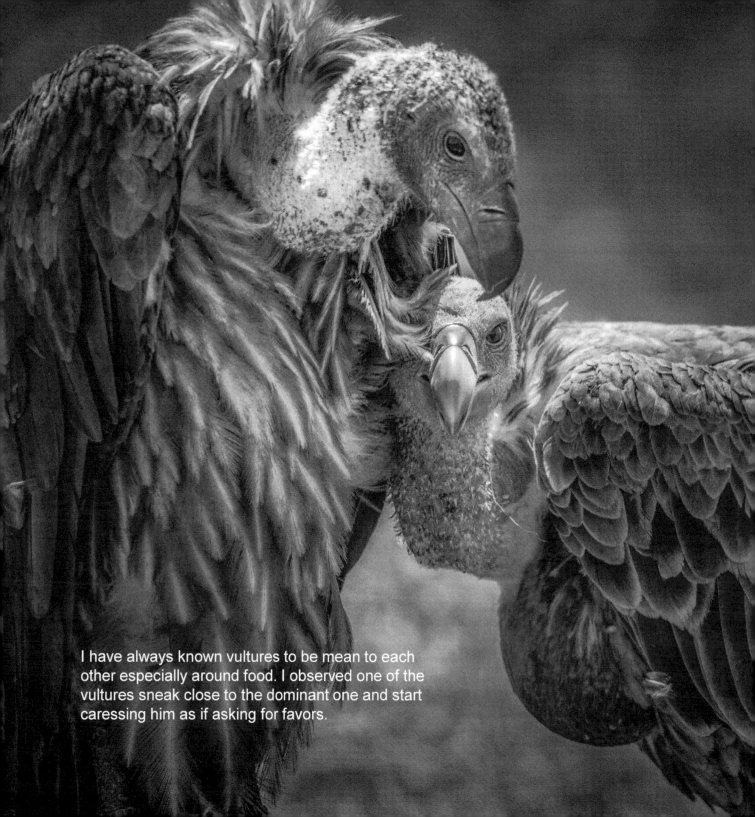

I have always known vultures to be mean to each other especially around food. I observed one of the vultures sneak close to the dominant one and start caressing him as if asking for favors.

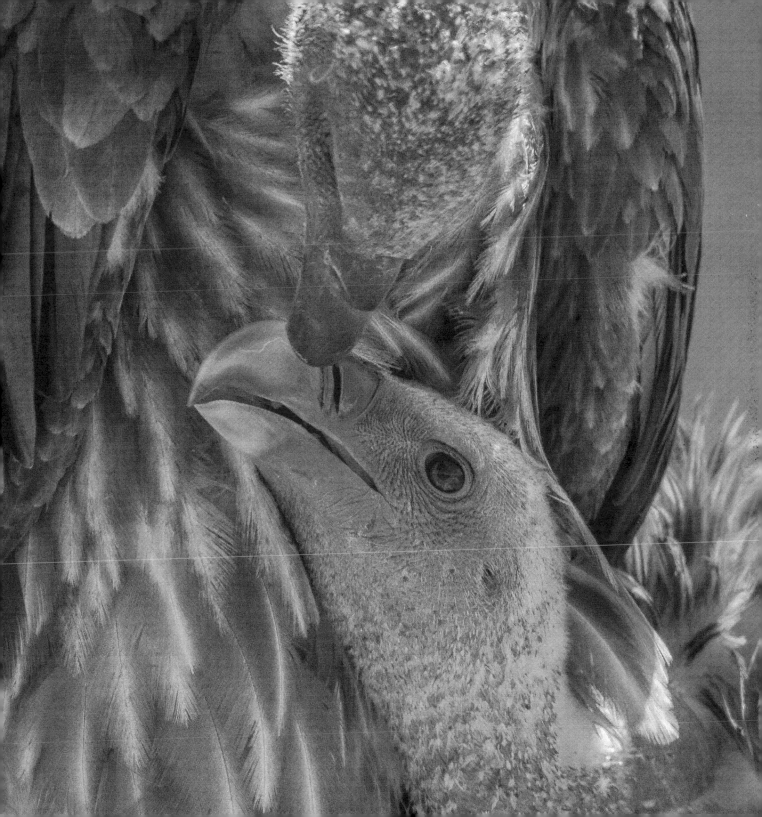

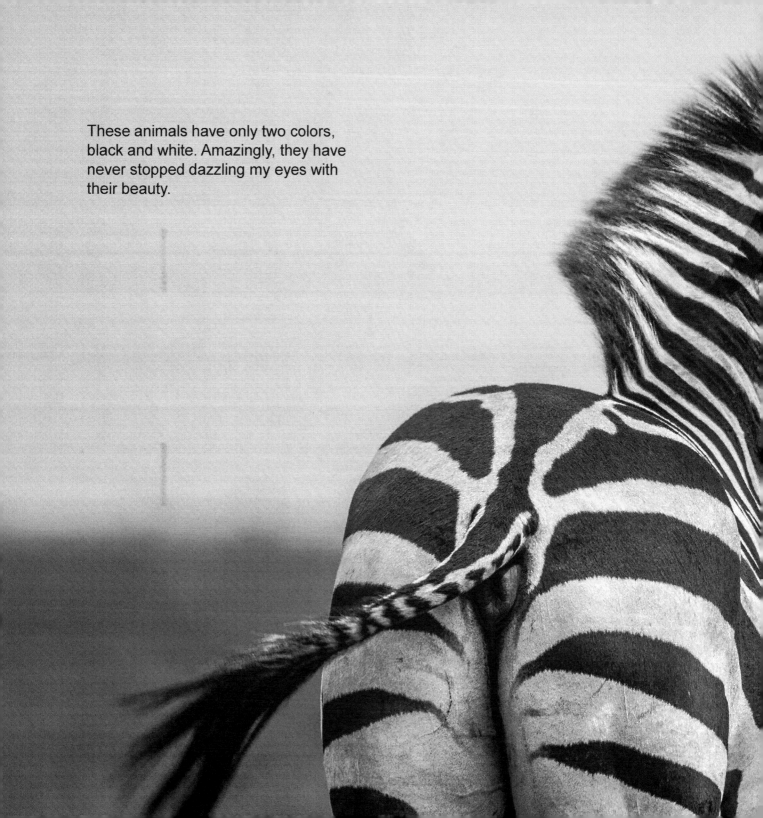

These animals have only two colors, black and white. Amazingly, they have never stopped dazzling my eyes with their beauty.

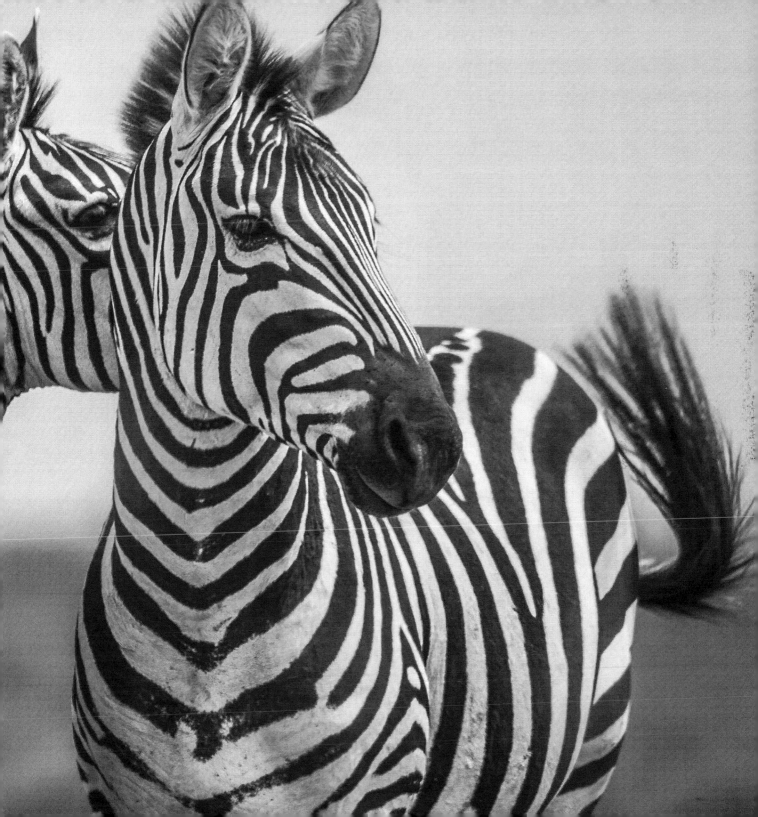

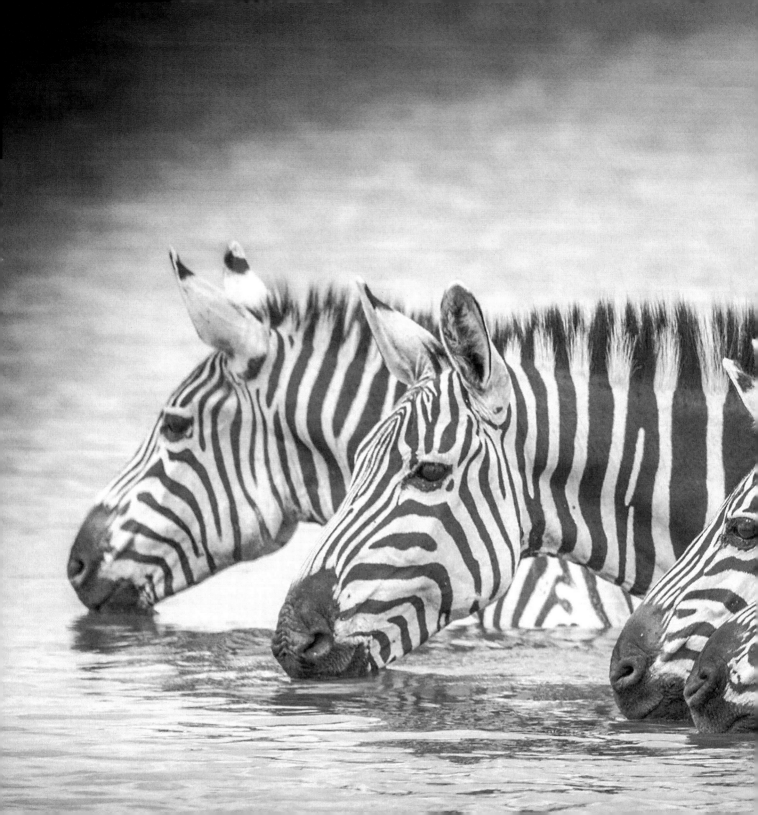

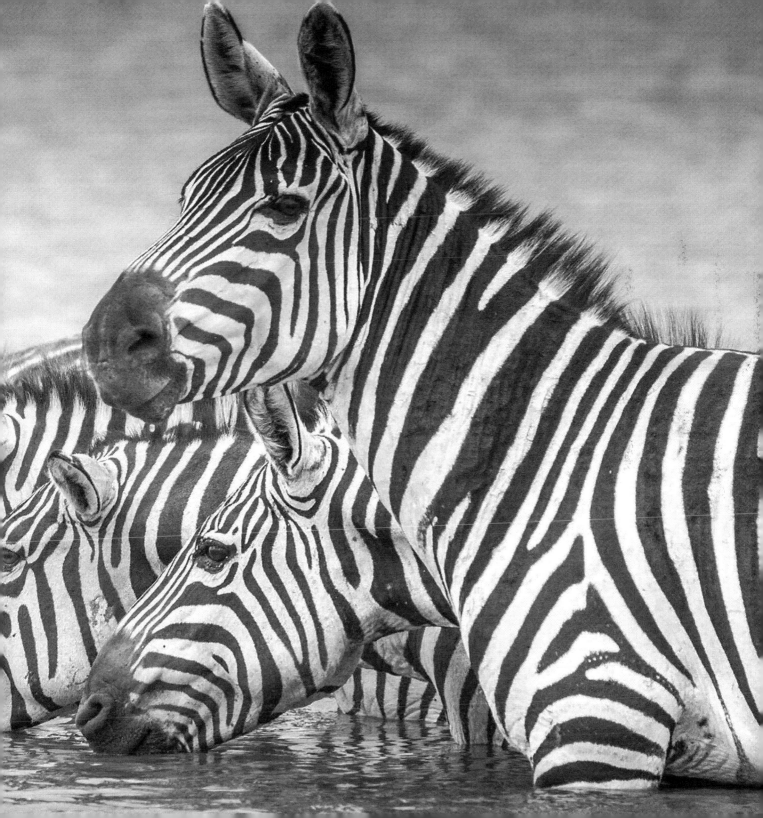

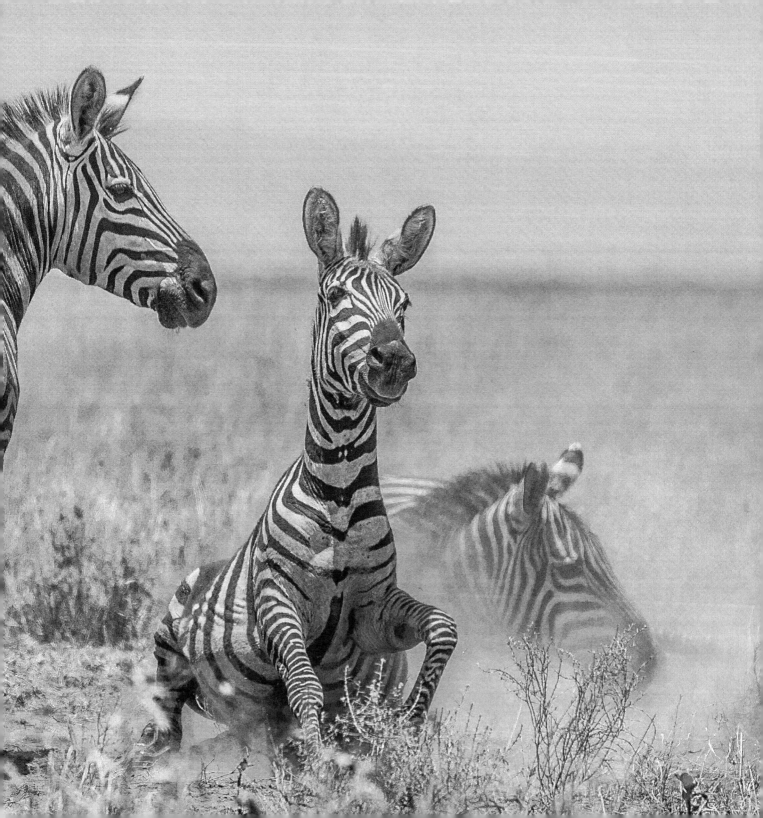

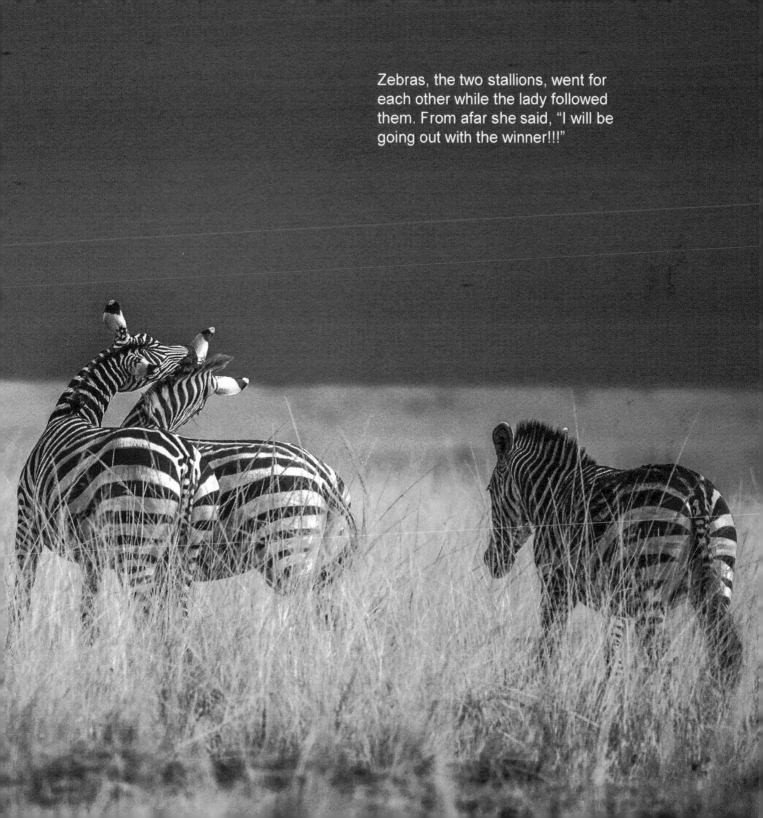

Zebras, the two stallions, went for each other while the lady followed them. From afar she said, "I will be going out with the winner!!!"

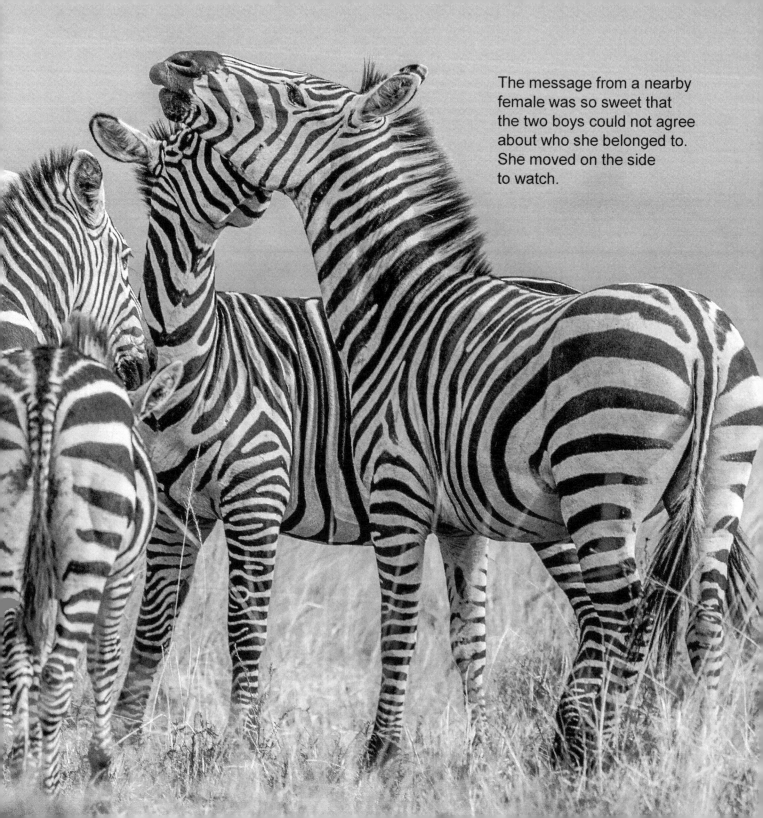

The message from a nearby female was so sweet that the two boys could not agree about who she belonged to. She moved on the side to watch.

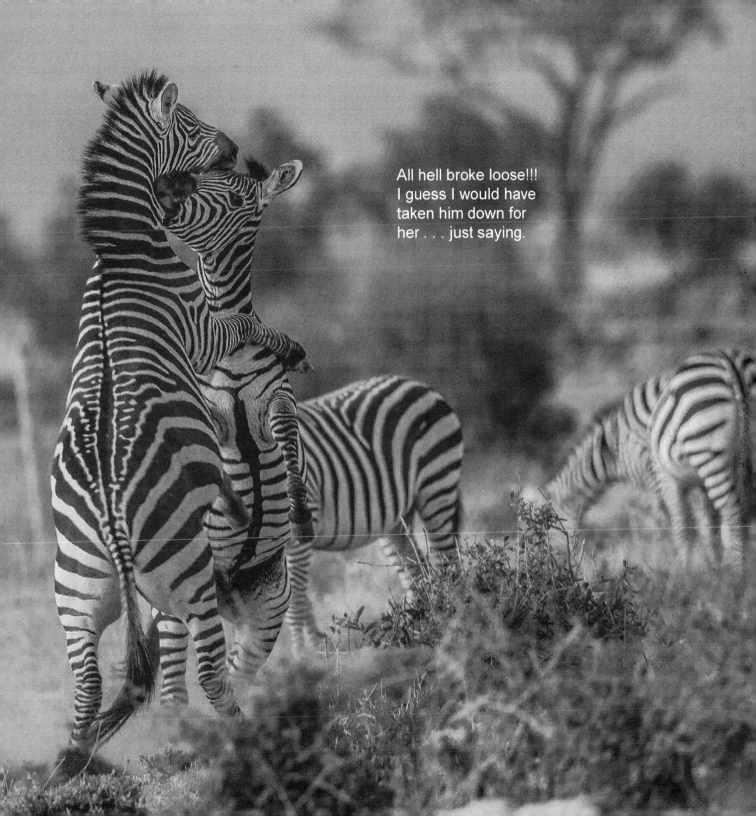

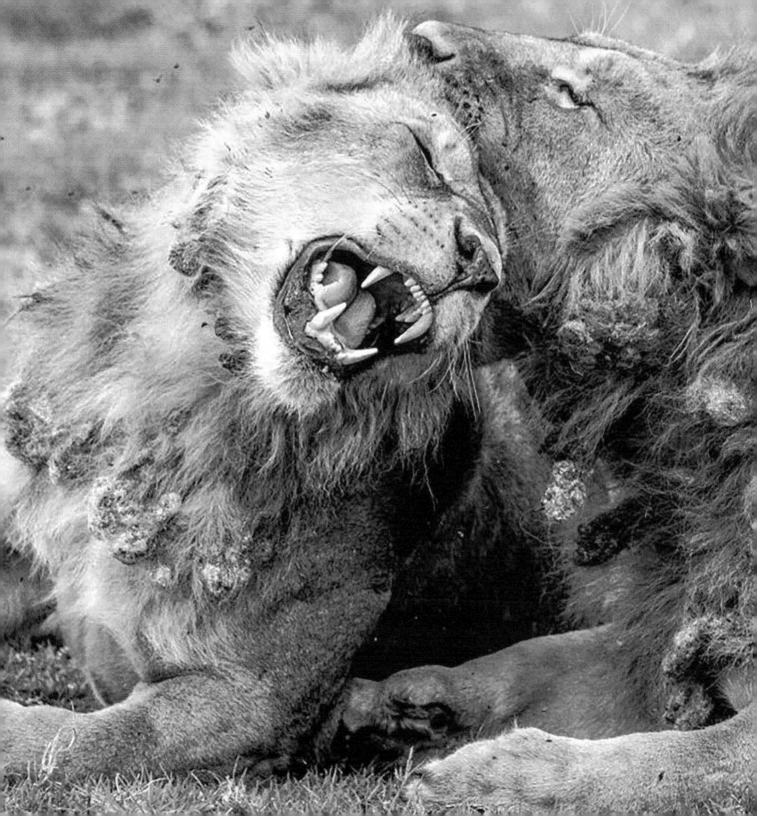

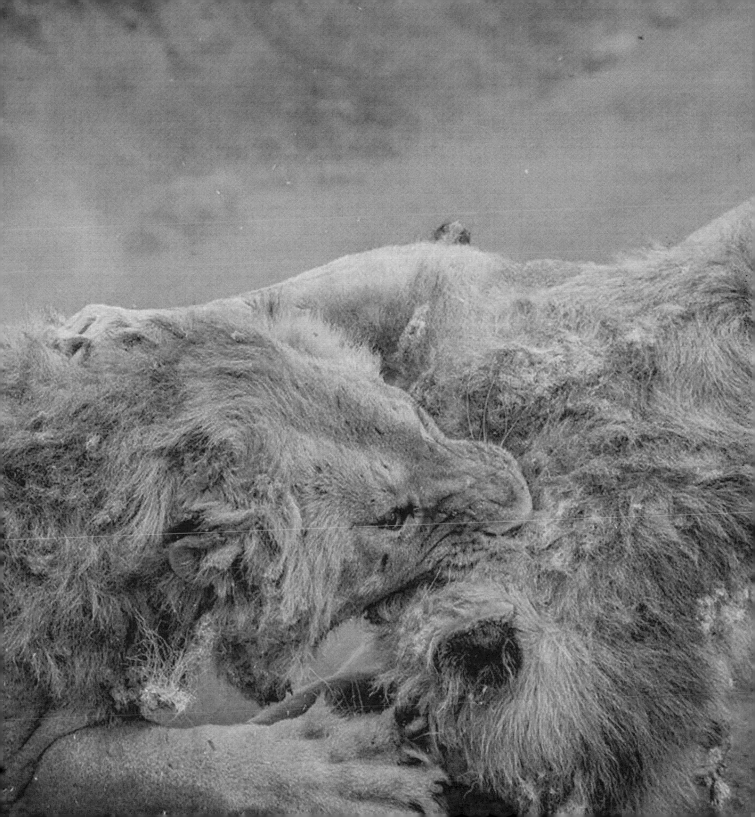

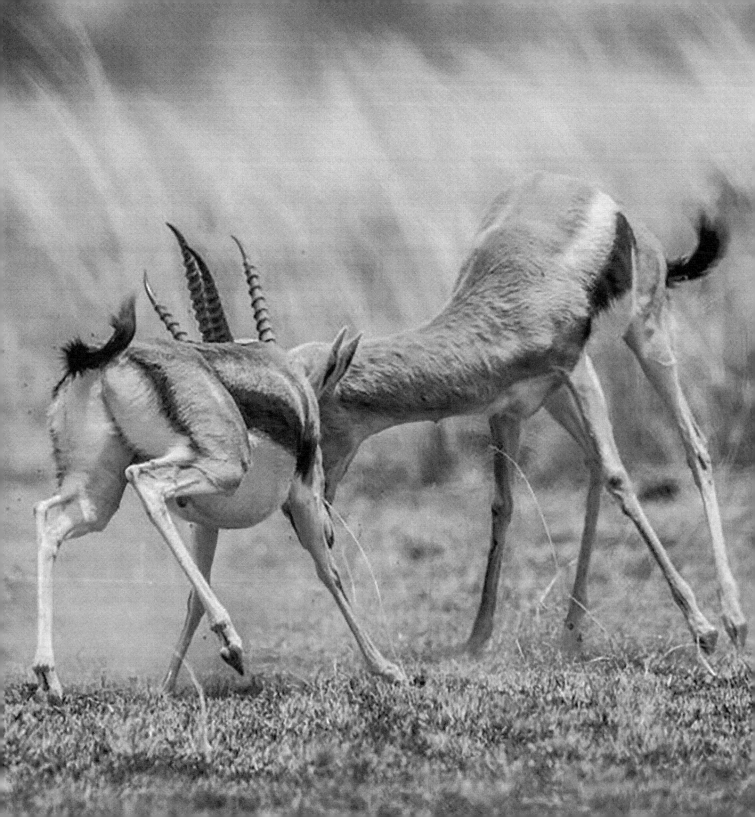

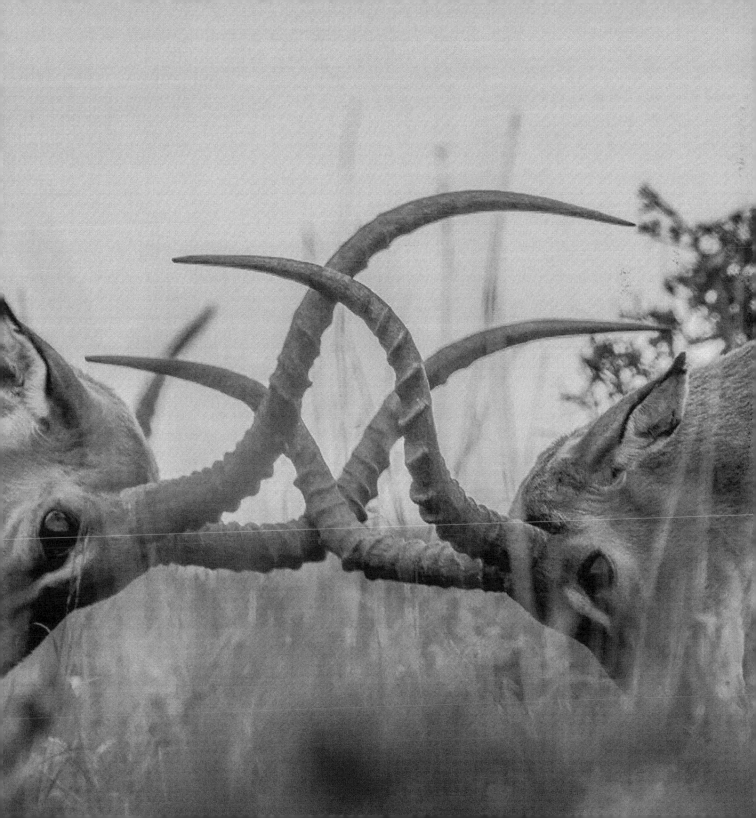

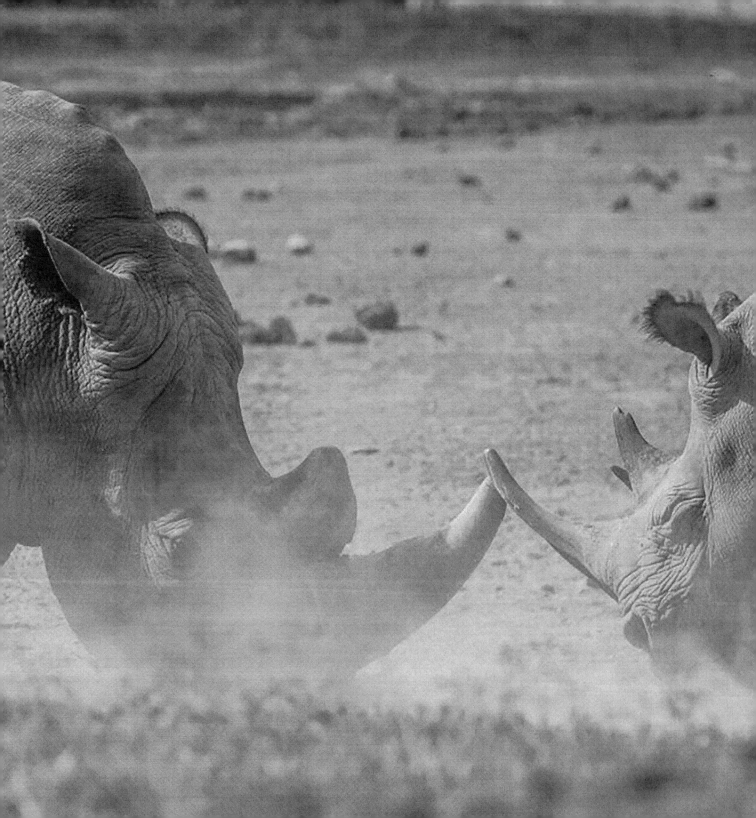

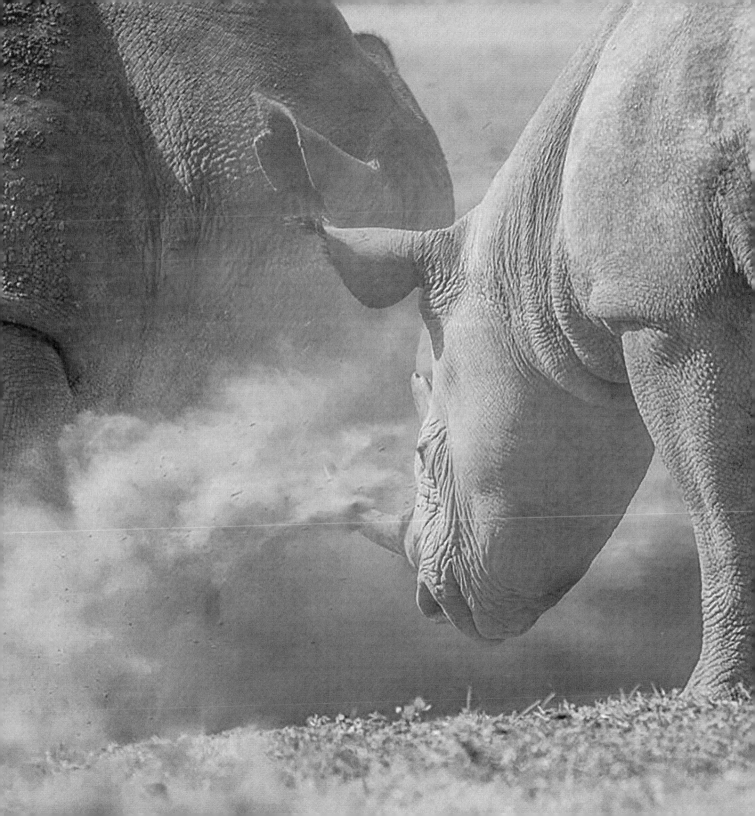

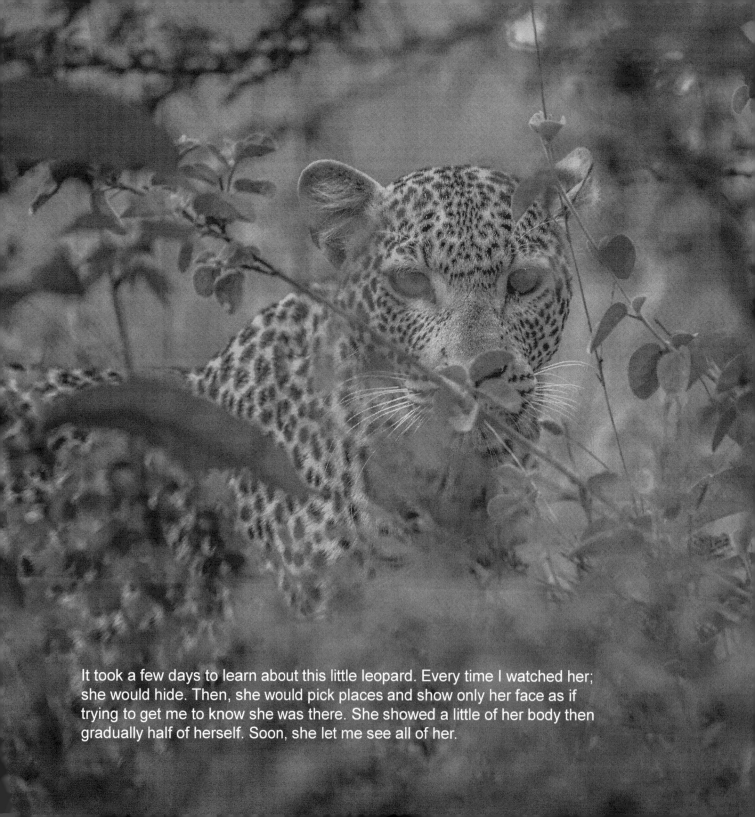

It took a few days to learn about this little leopard. Every time I watched her; she would hide. Then, she would pick places and show only her face as if trying to get me to know she was there. She showed a little of her body then gradually half of herself. Soon, she let me see all of her.

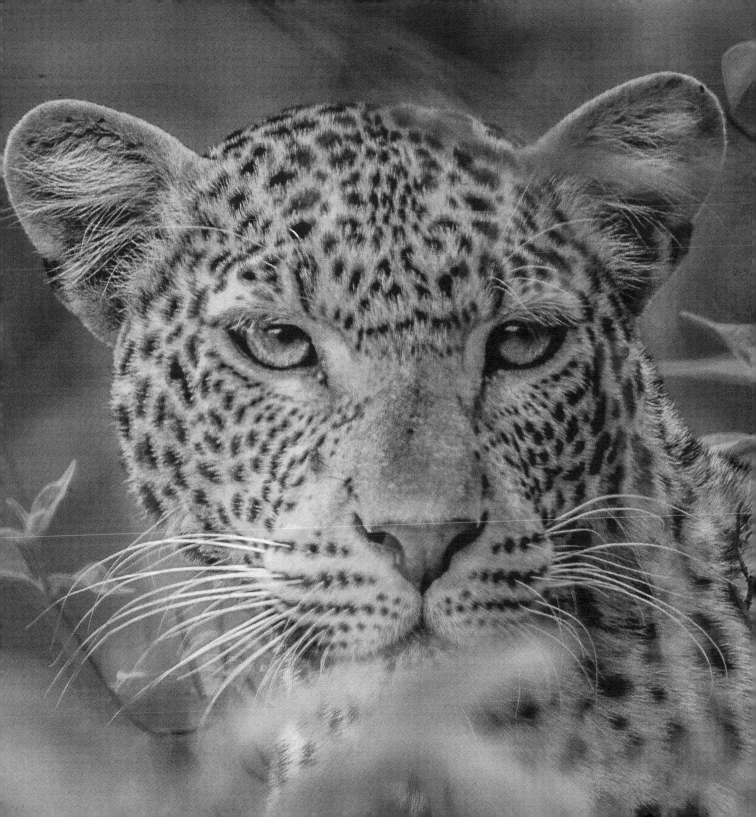

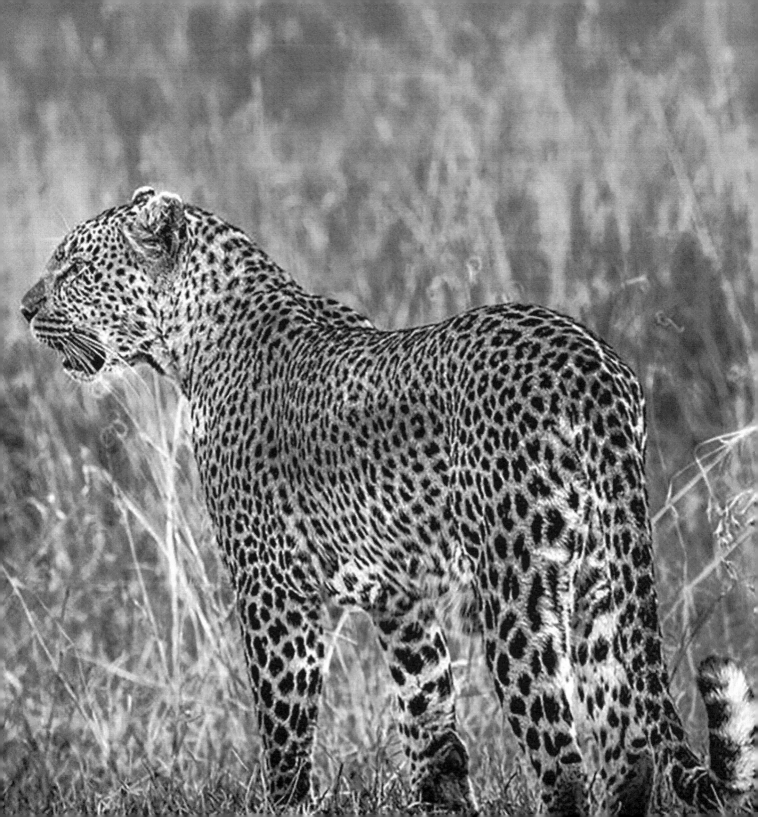

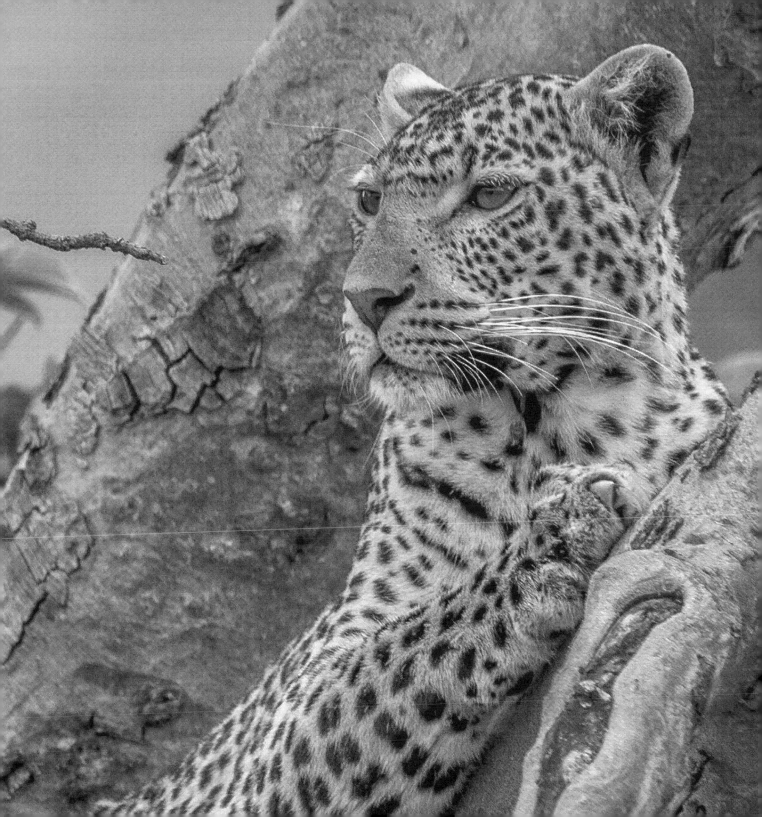

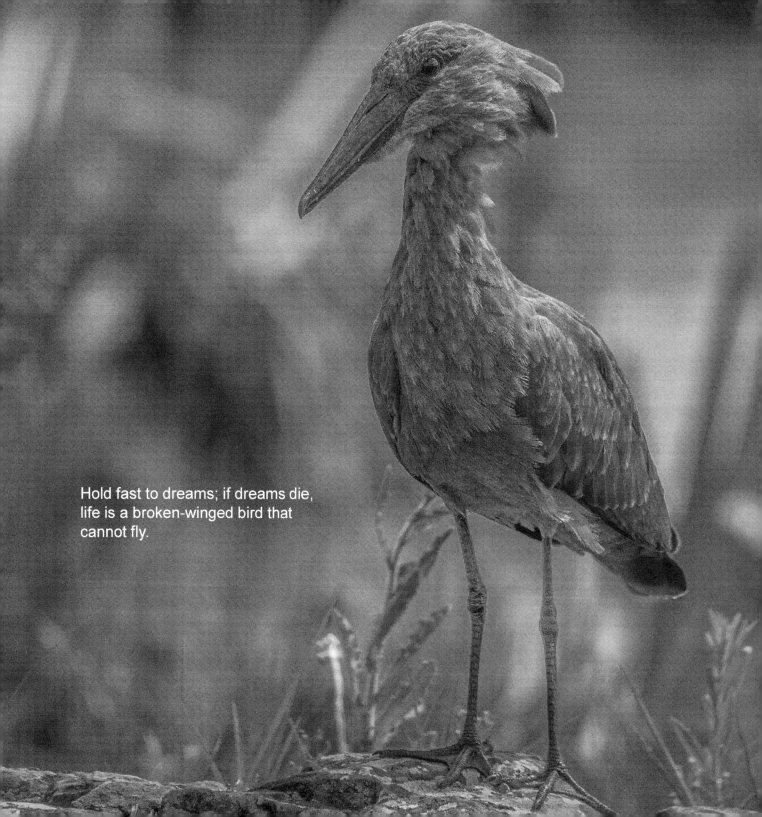

Hold fast to dreams; if dreams die,
life is a broken-winged bird that
cannot fly.

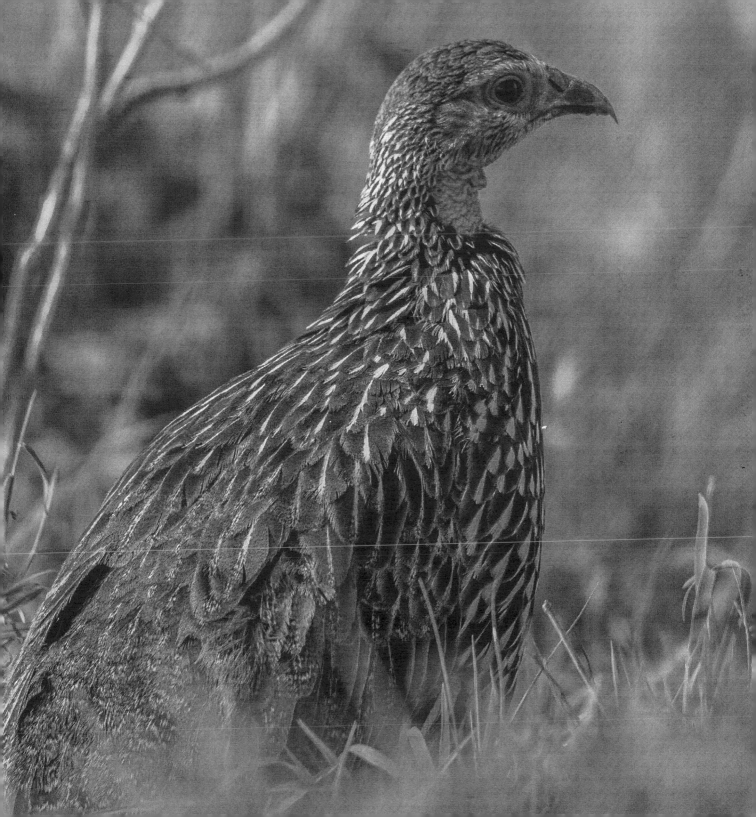

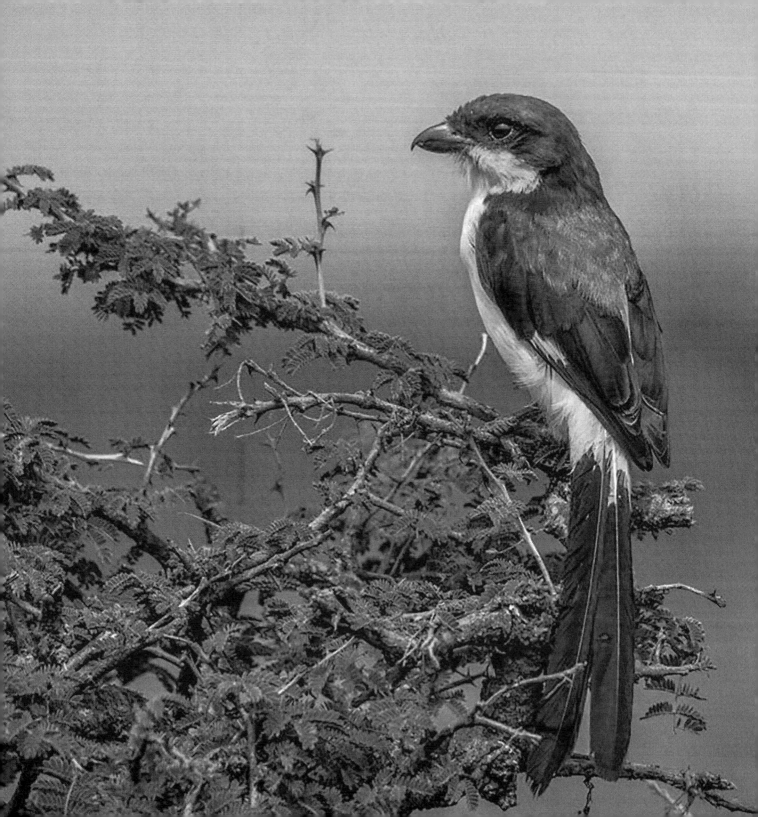

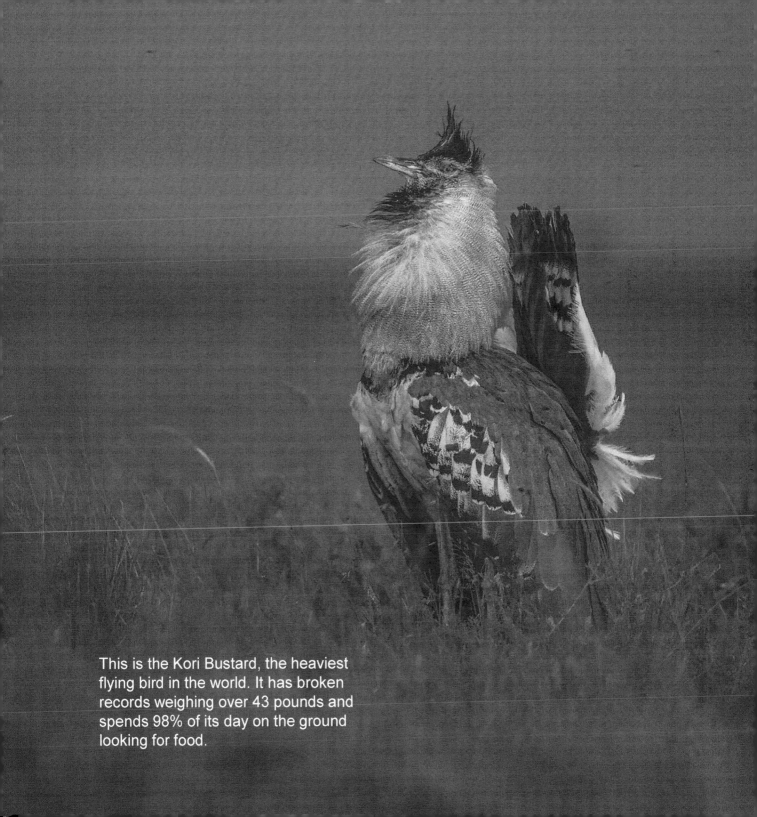

This is the Kori Bustard, the heaviest flying bird in the world. It has broken records weighing over 43 pounds and spends 98% of its day on the ground looking for food.

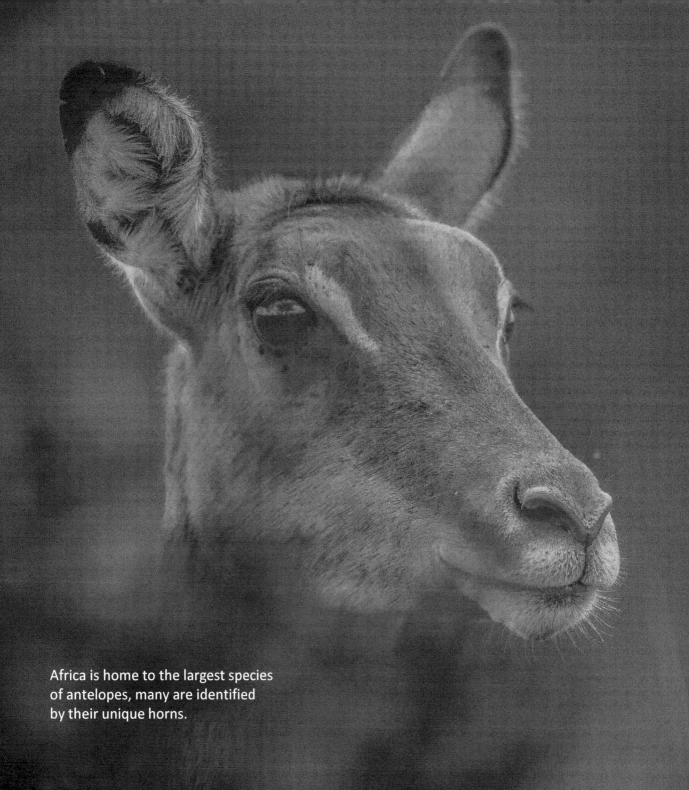

Africa is home to the largest species of antelopes, many are identified by their unique horns.

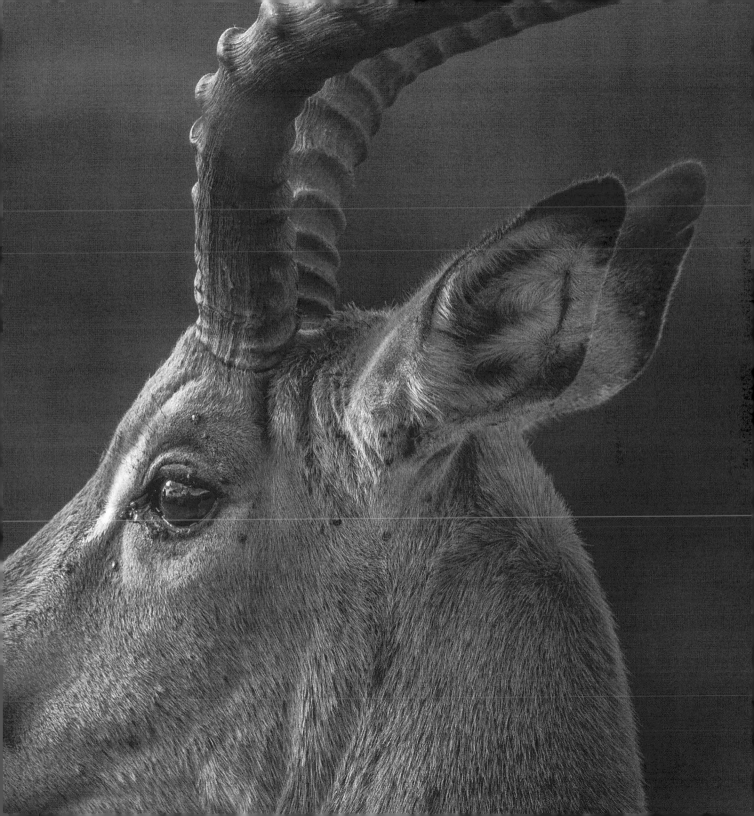

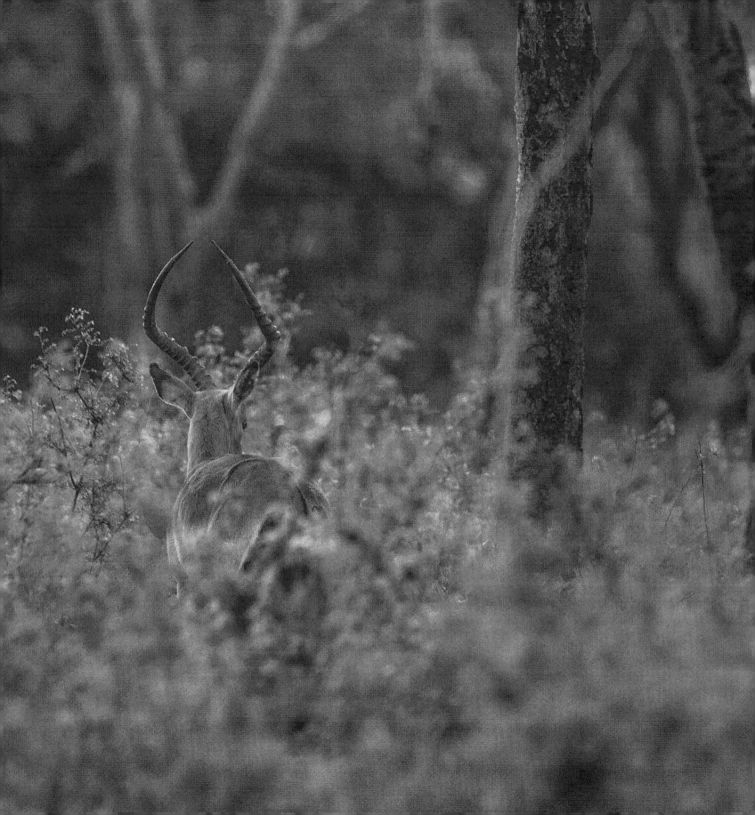

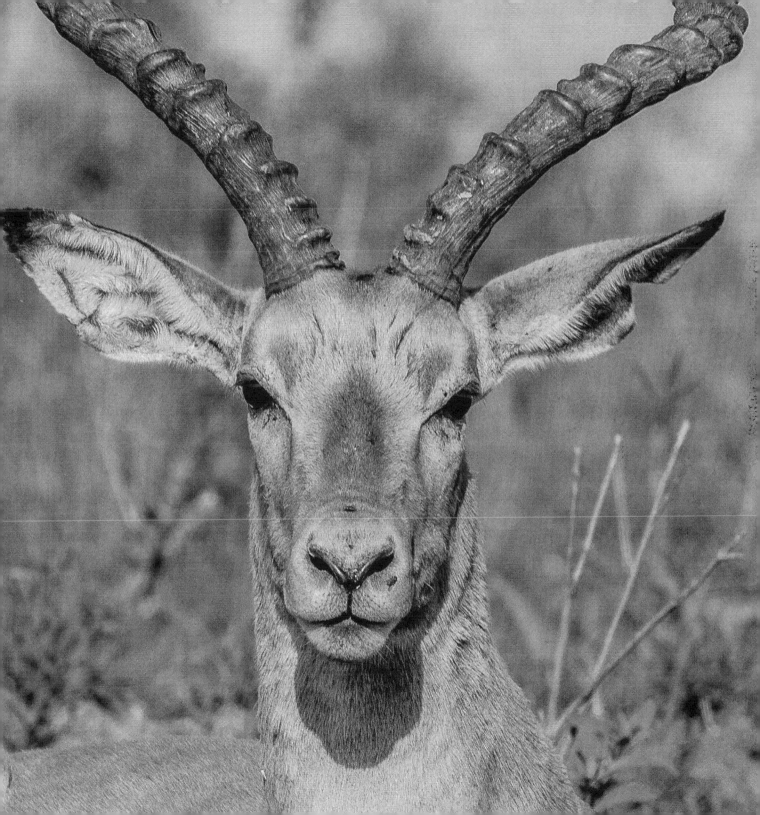

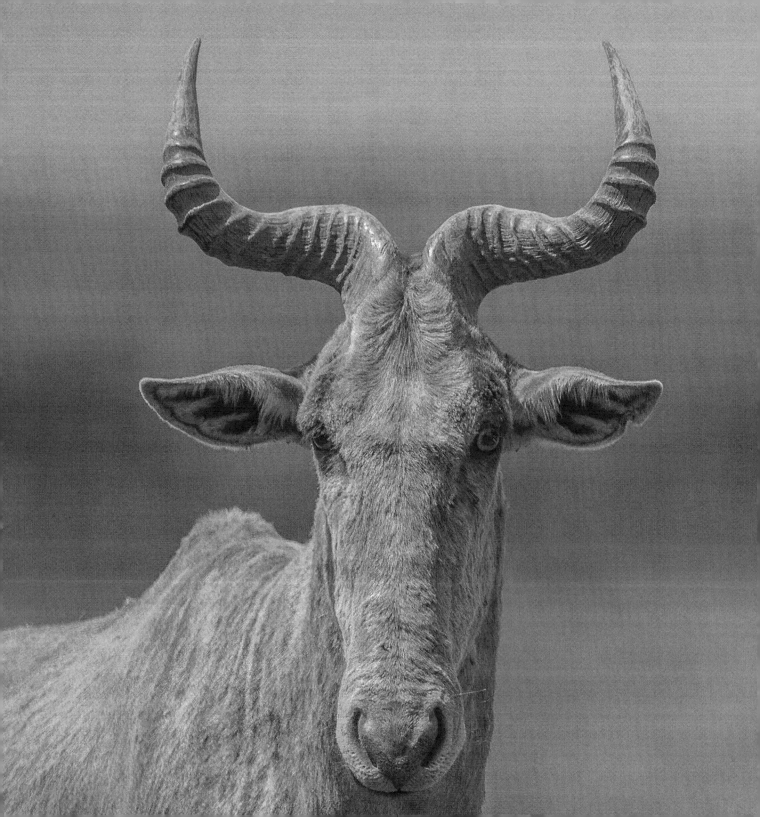

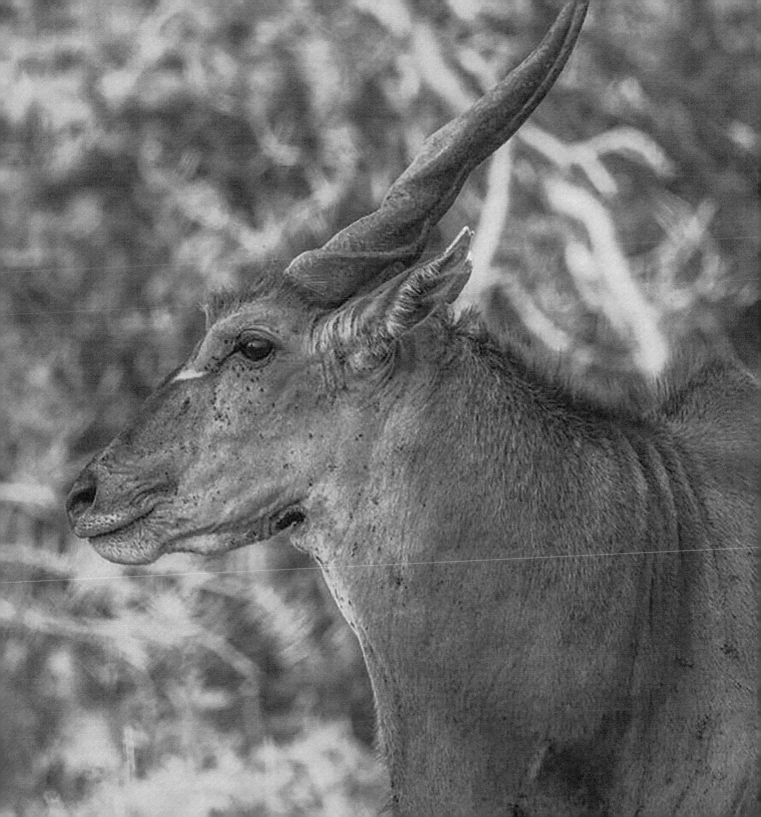

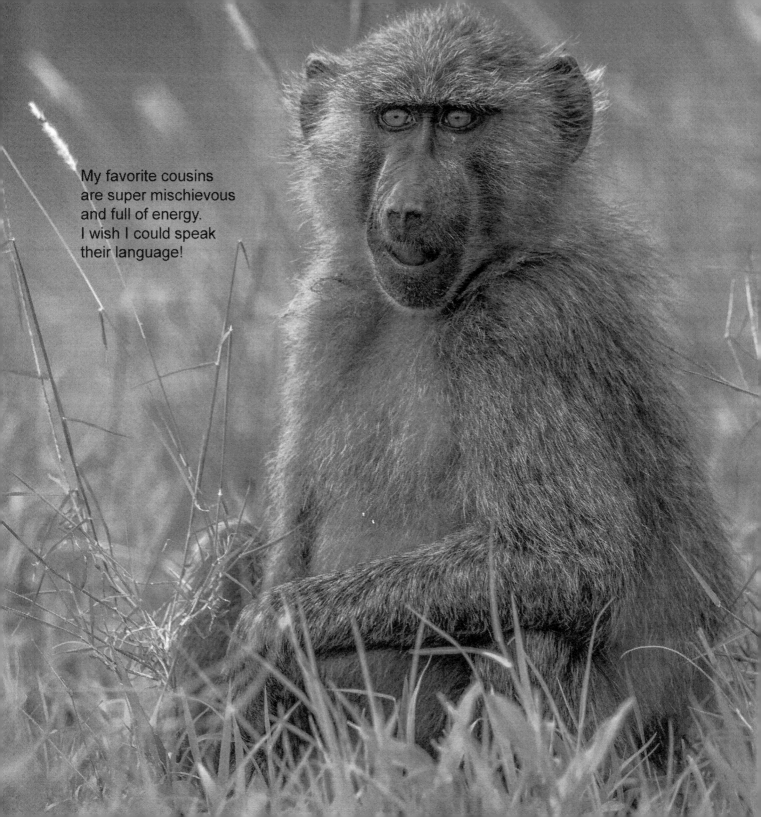

My favorite cousins
are super mischievous
and full of energy.
I wish I could speak
their language!

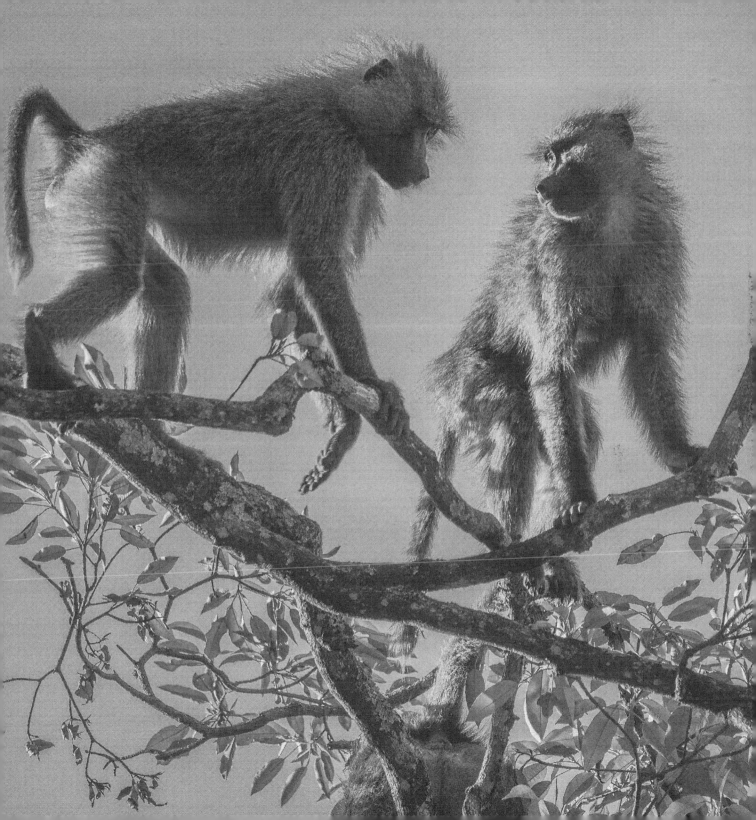

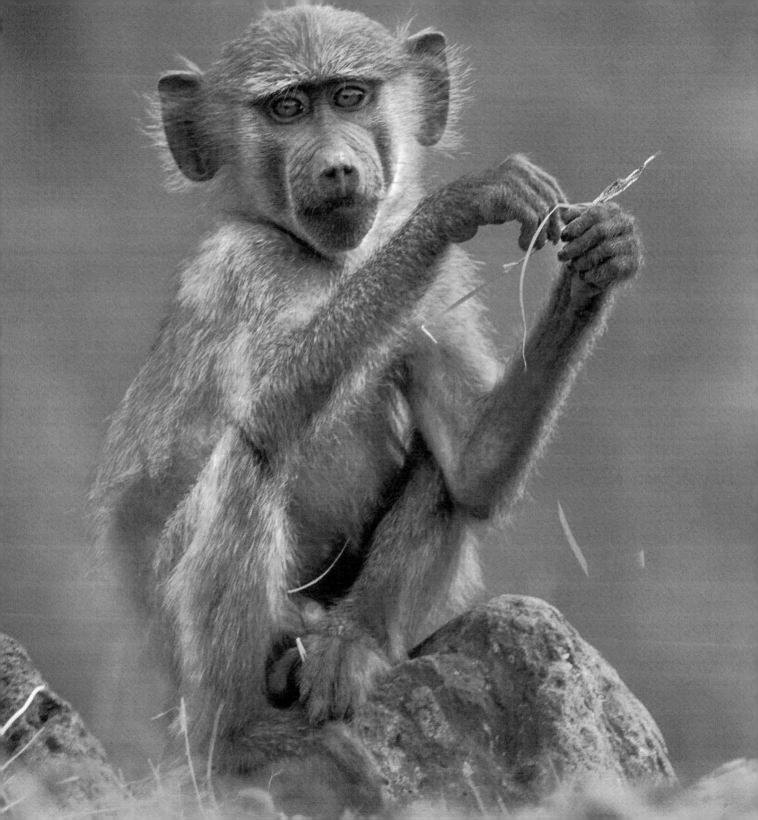

I watch animals moving, but not just moving. Their eyes stay focused on a target. Sometimes other animals (and me trying to get a piece of the action) are close enough to ruin their plans. But, noooooo! They stay focused on the target and getting what they want.

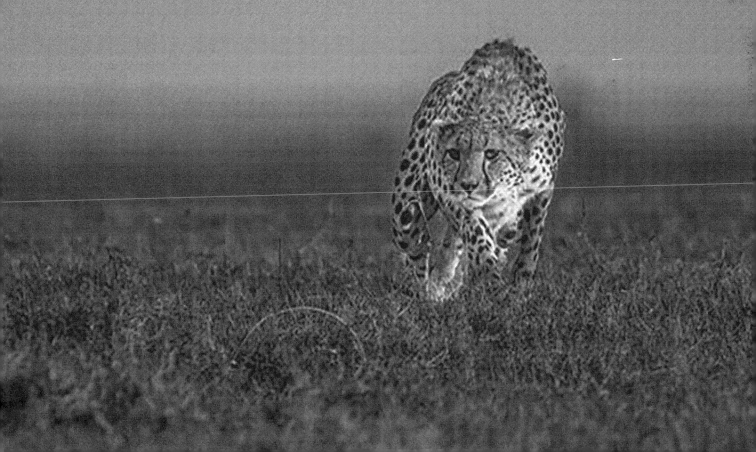

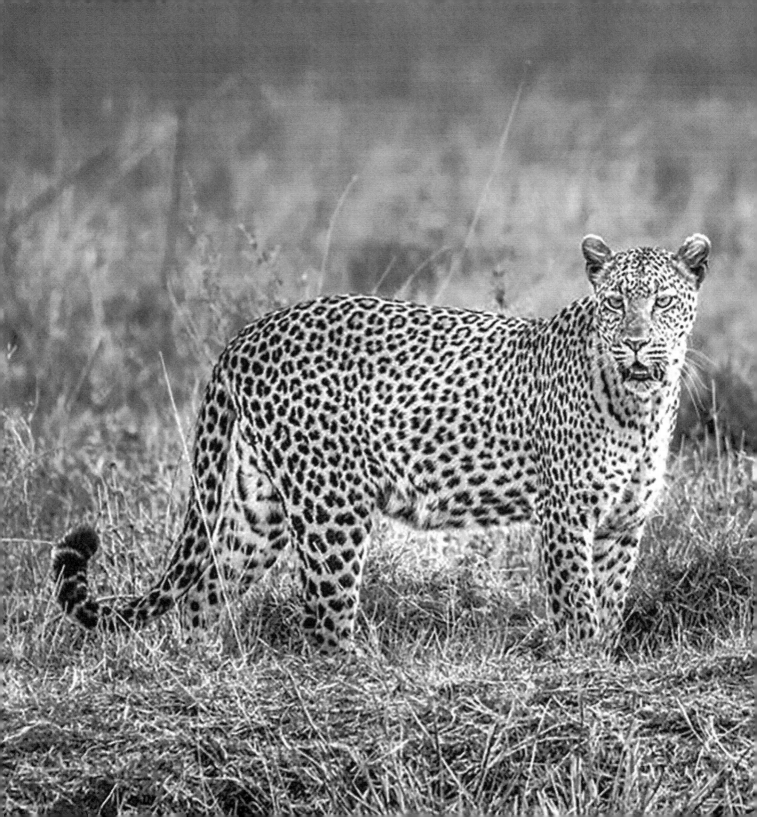

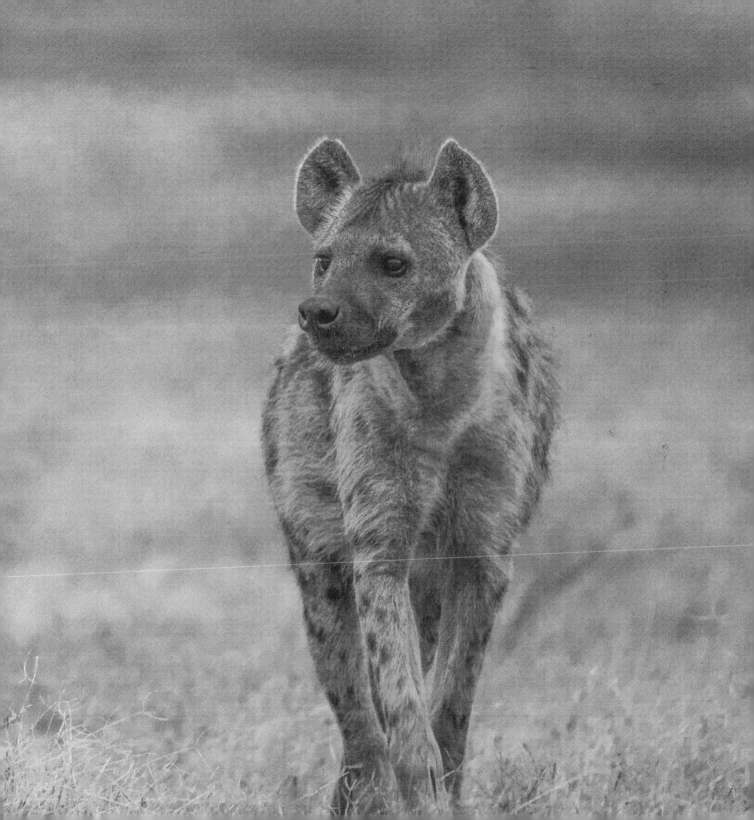

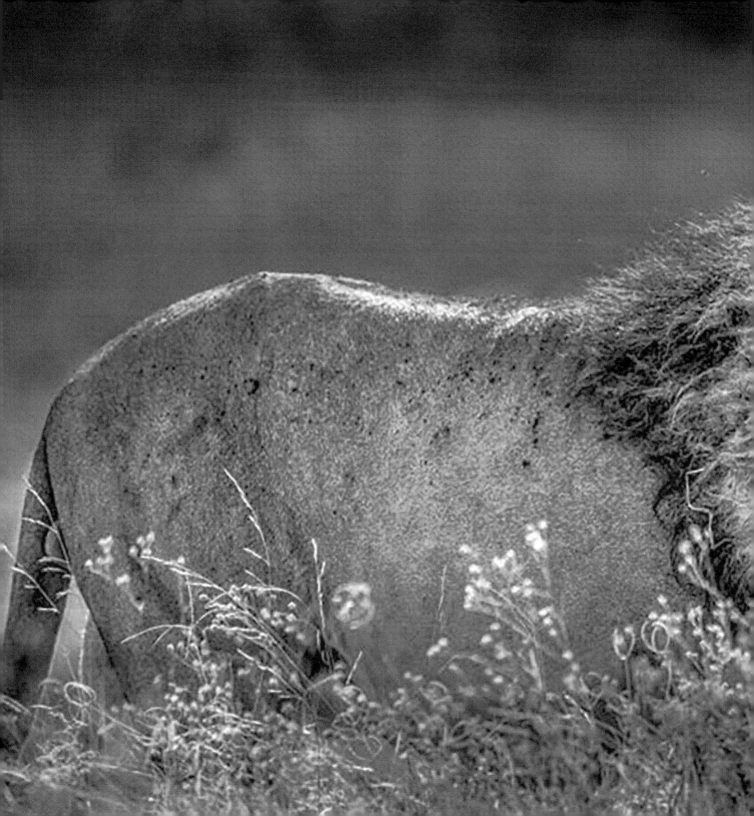

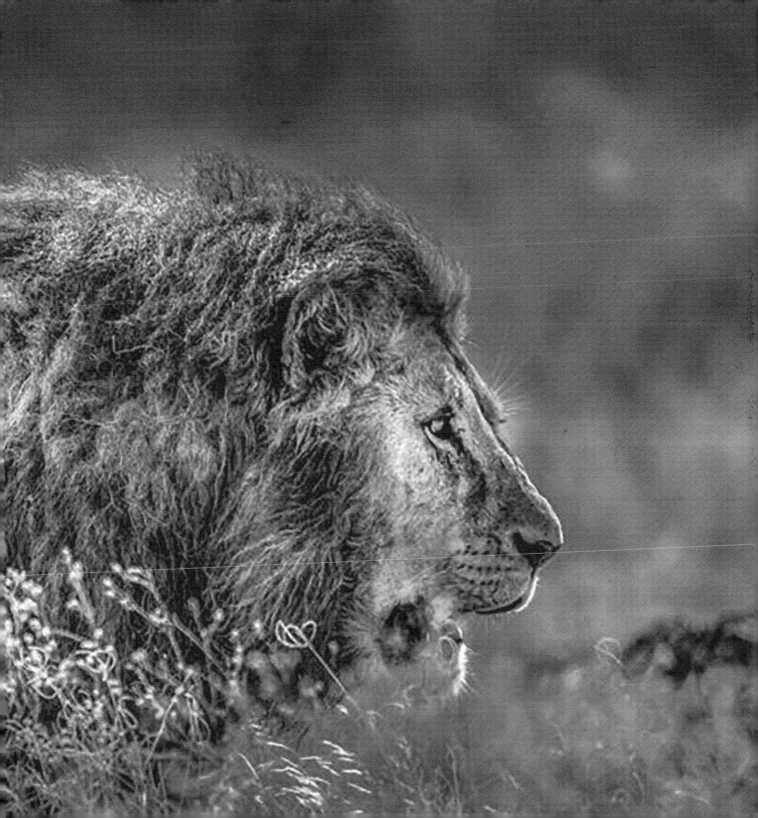

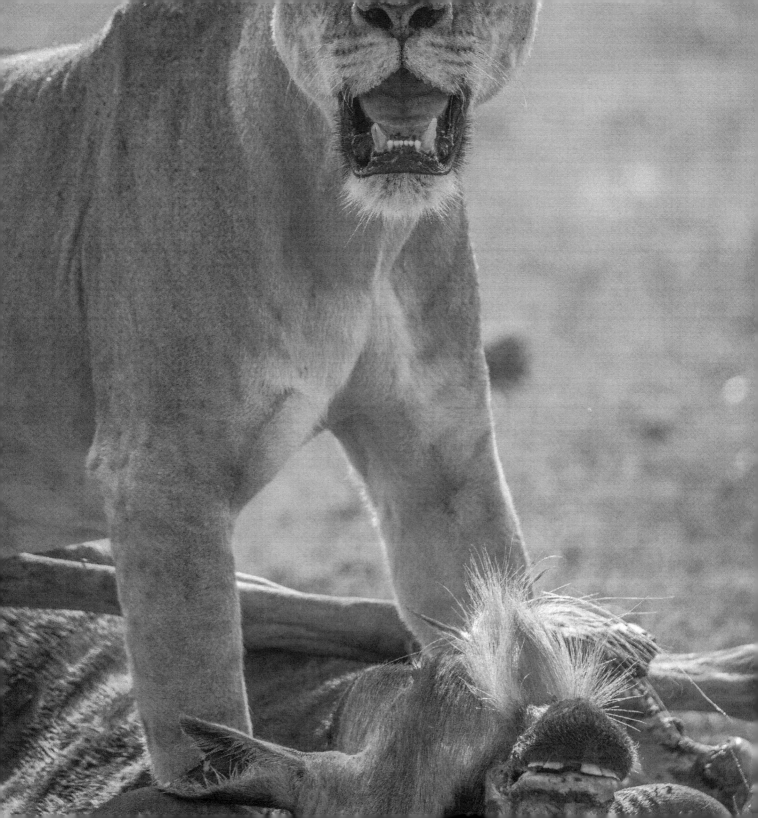

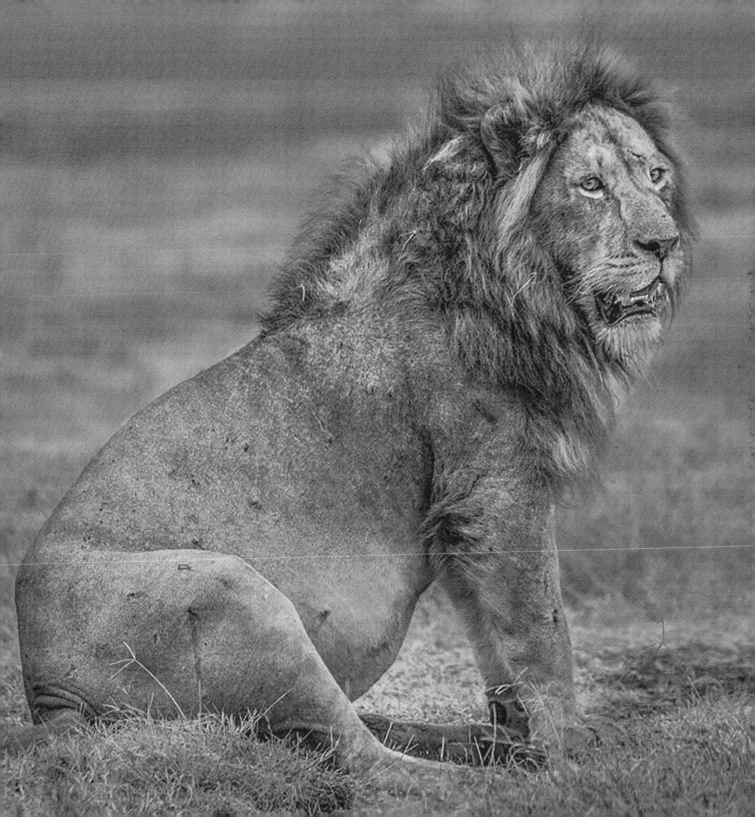

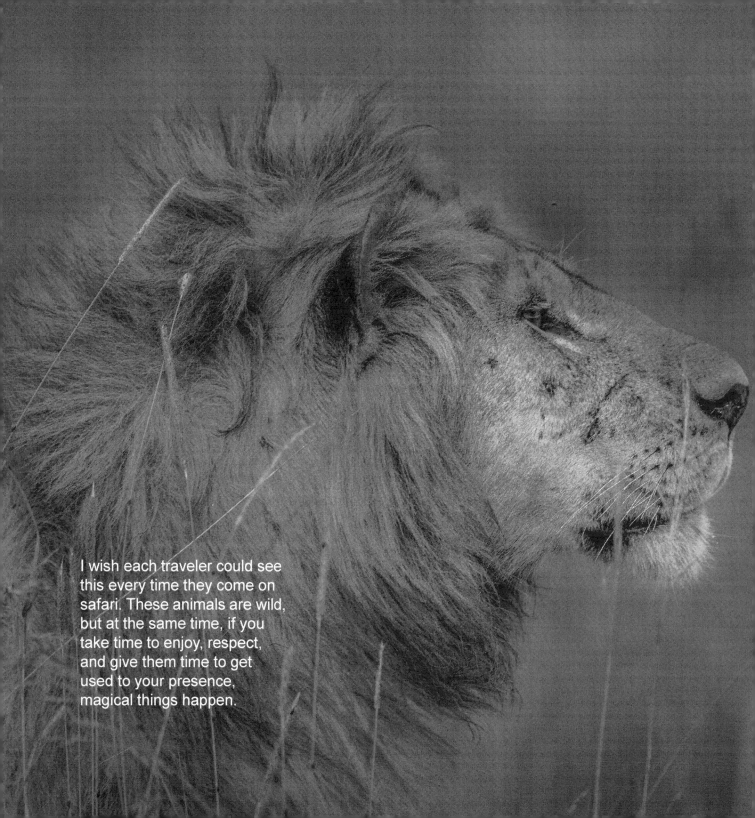

I wish each traveler could see this every time they come on safari. These animals are wild, but at the same time, if you take time to enjoy, respect, and give them time to get used to your presence, magical things happen.

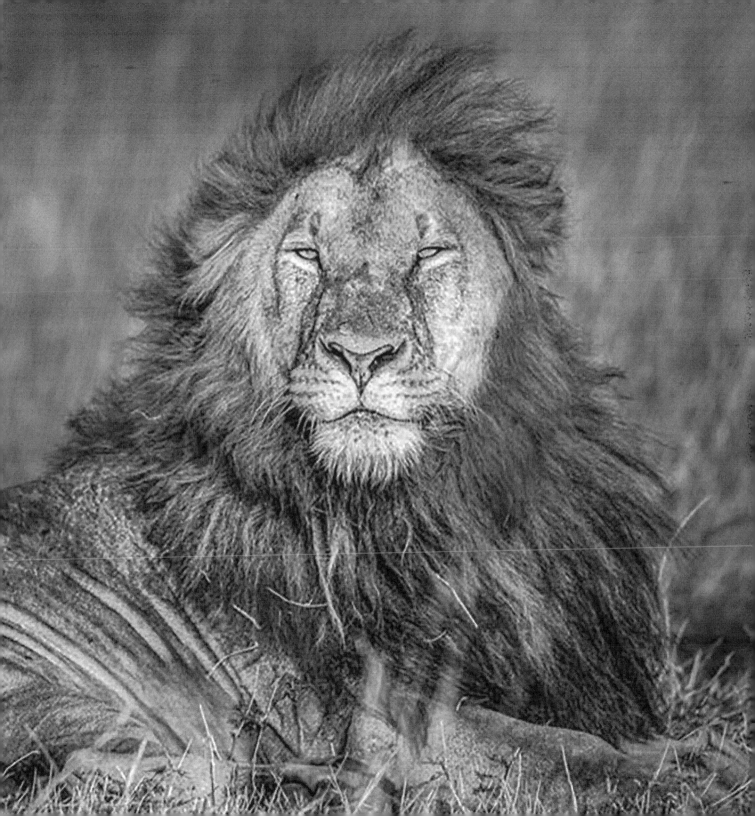

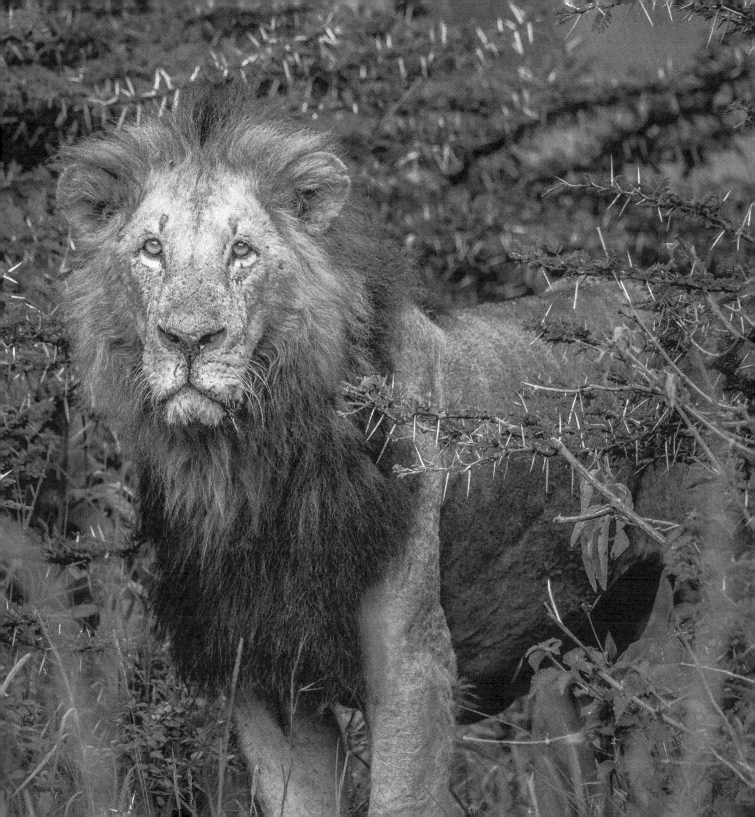

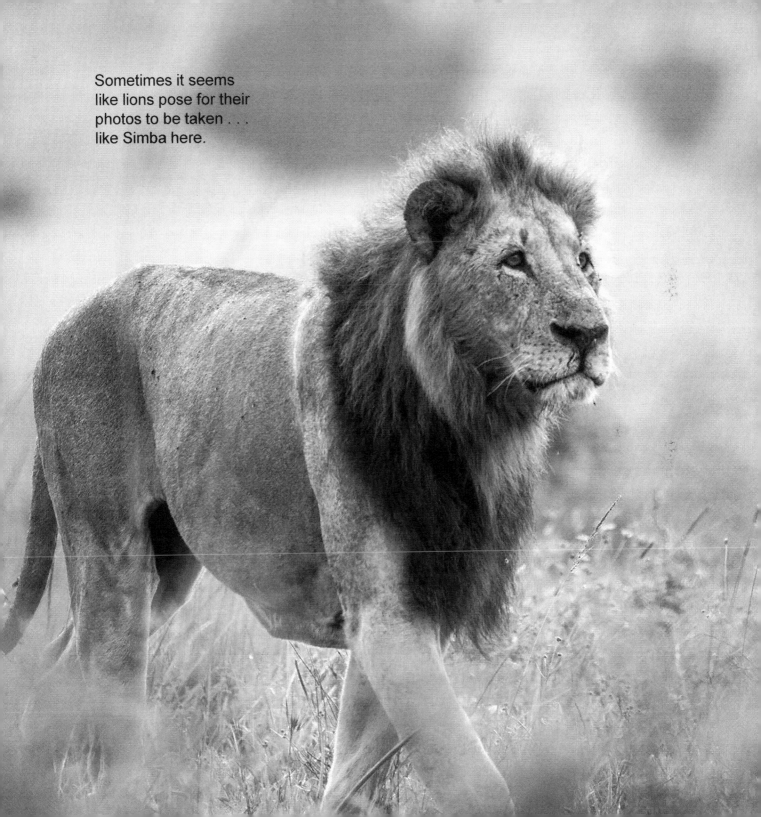

Sometimes it seems
like lions pose for their
photos to be taken . . .
like Simba here.

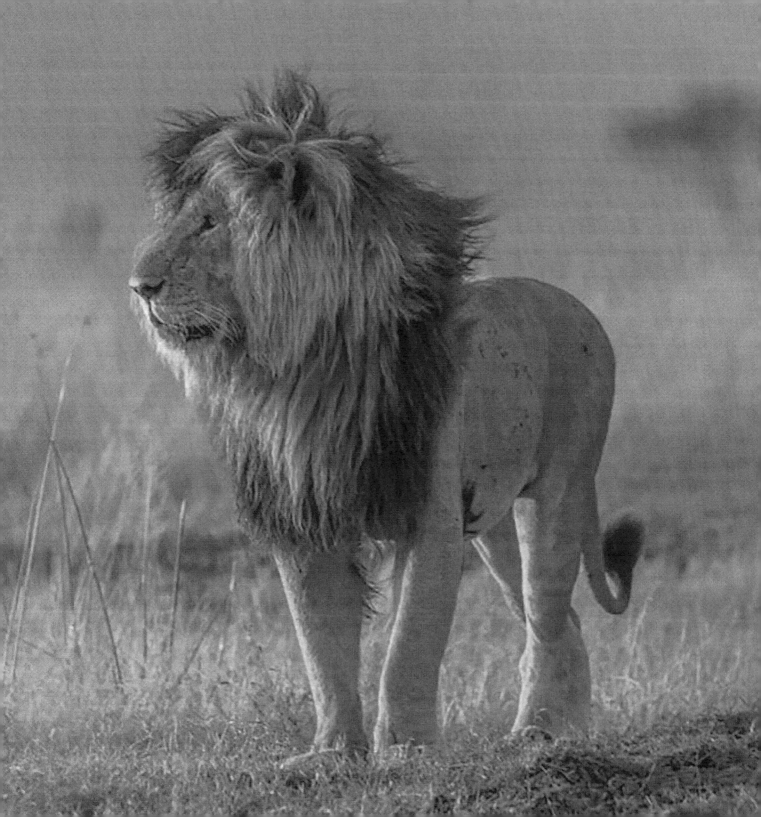

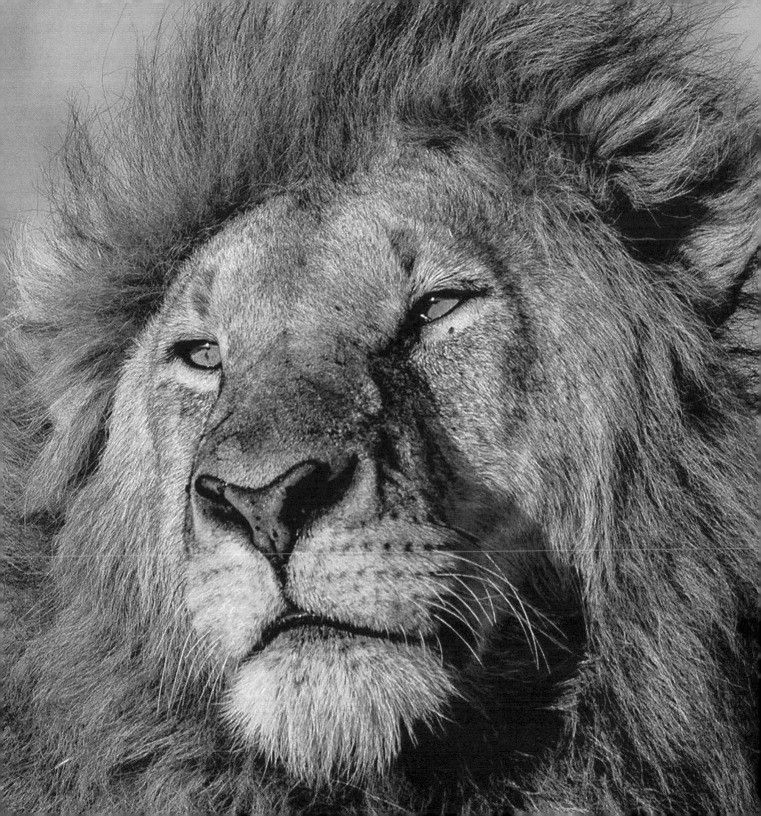

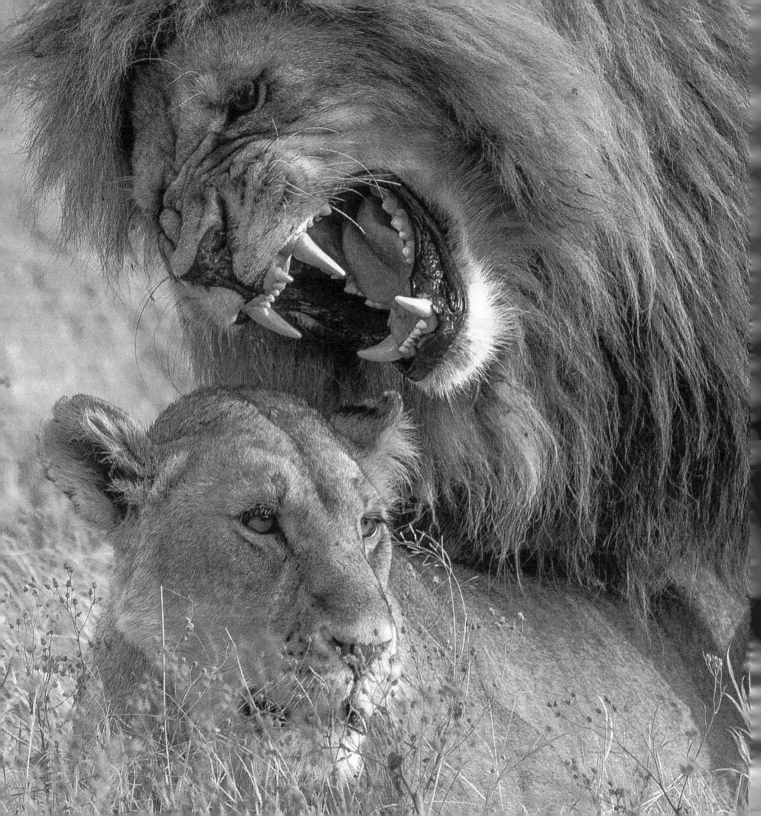

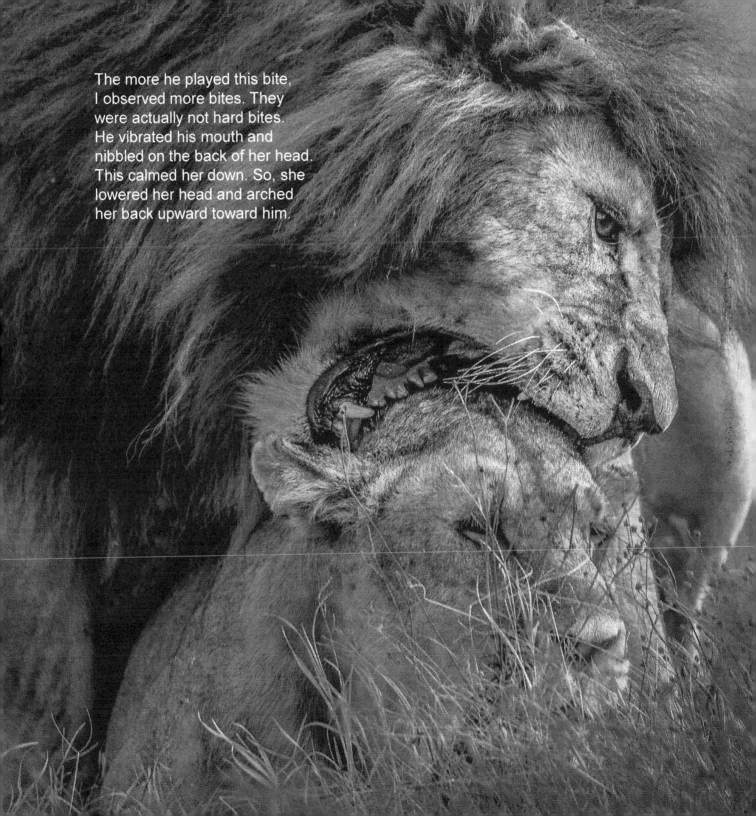

The more he played this bite, I observed more bites. They were actually not hard bites. He vibrated his mouth and nibbled on the back of her head. This calmed her down. So, she lowered her head and arched her back upward toward him.

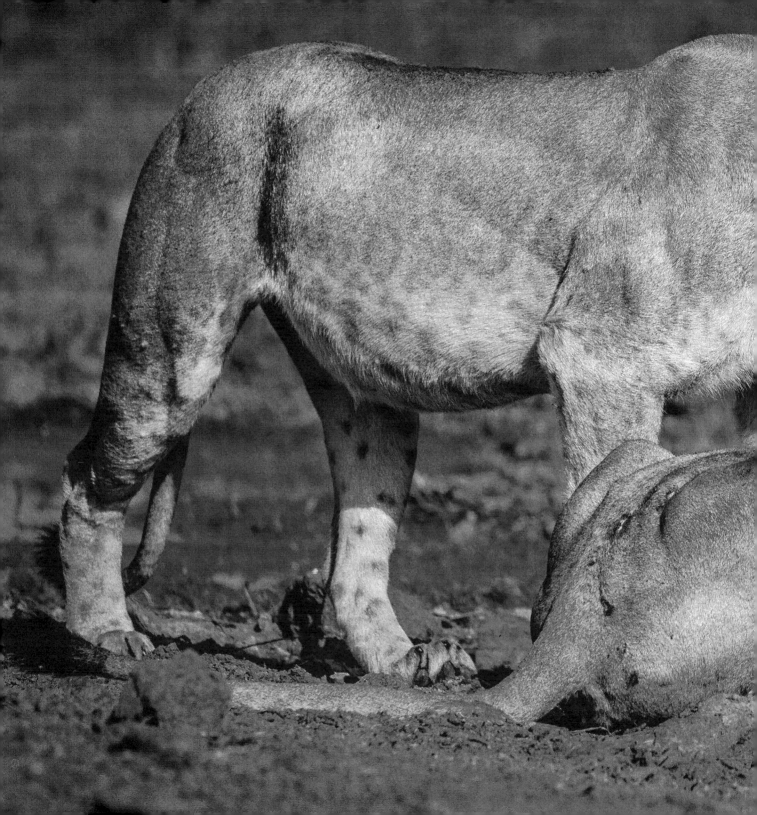

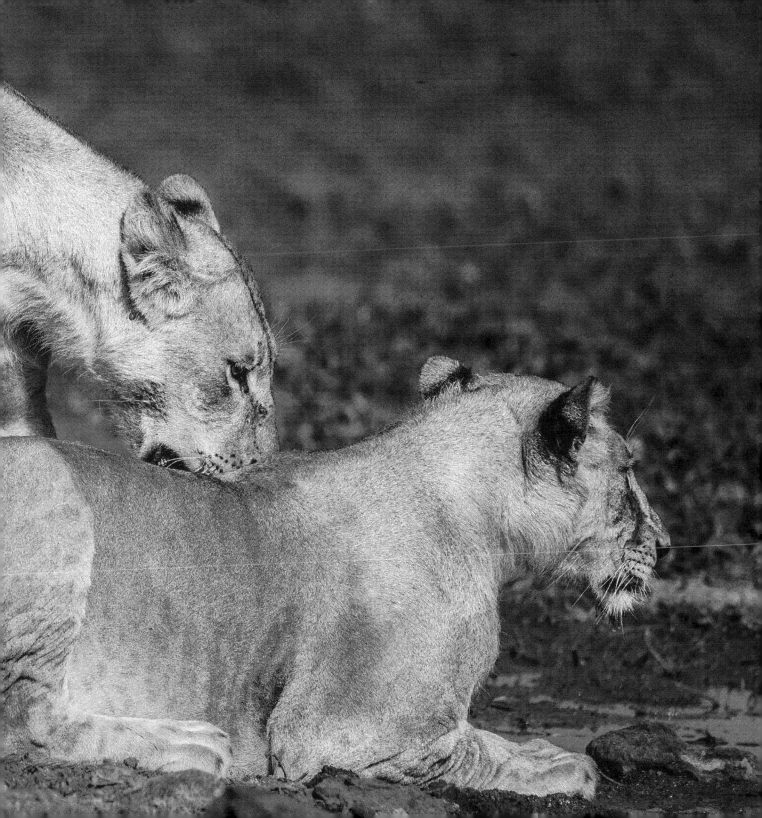

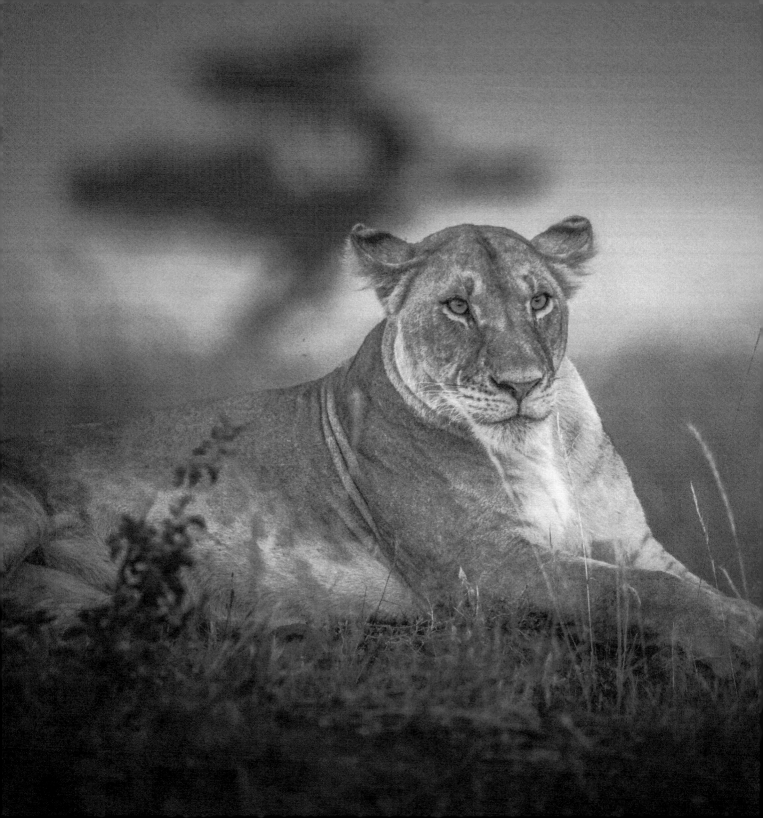

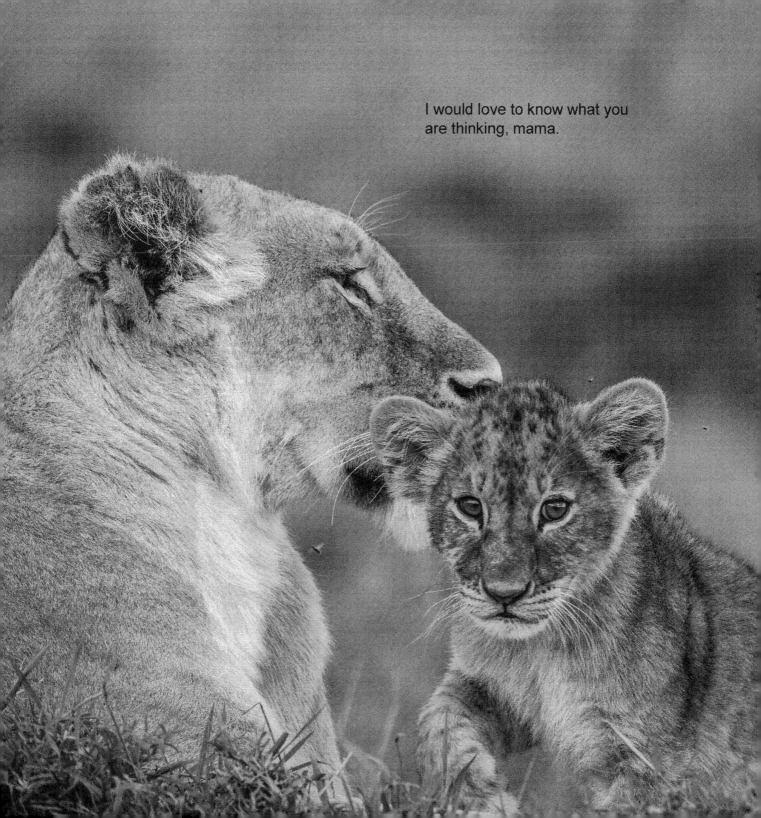

I would love to know what you are thinking, mama.

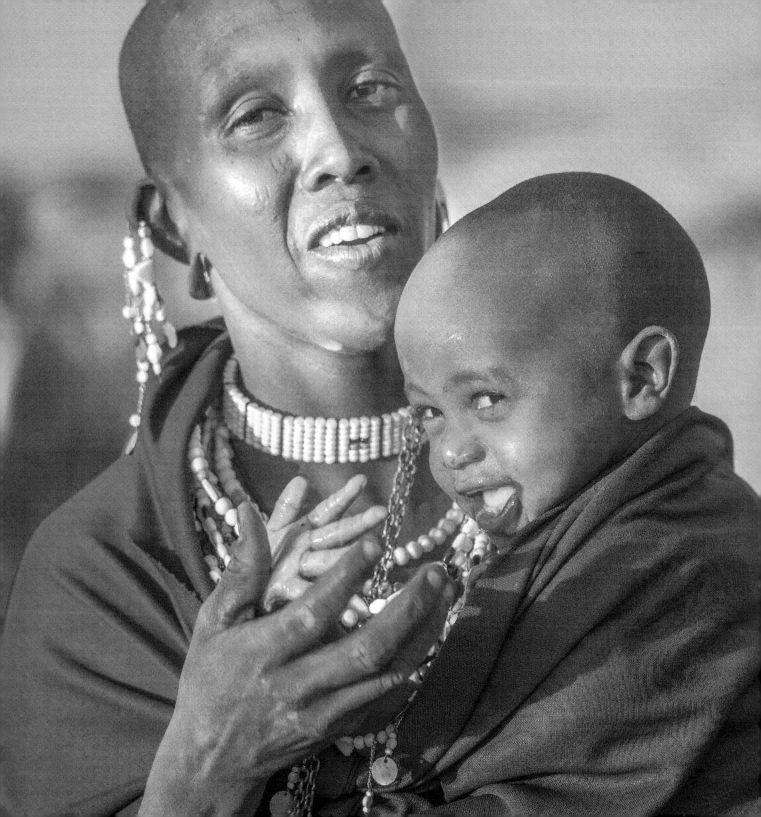

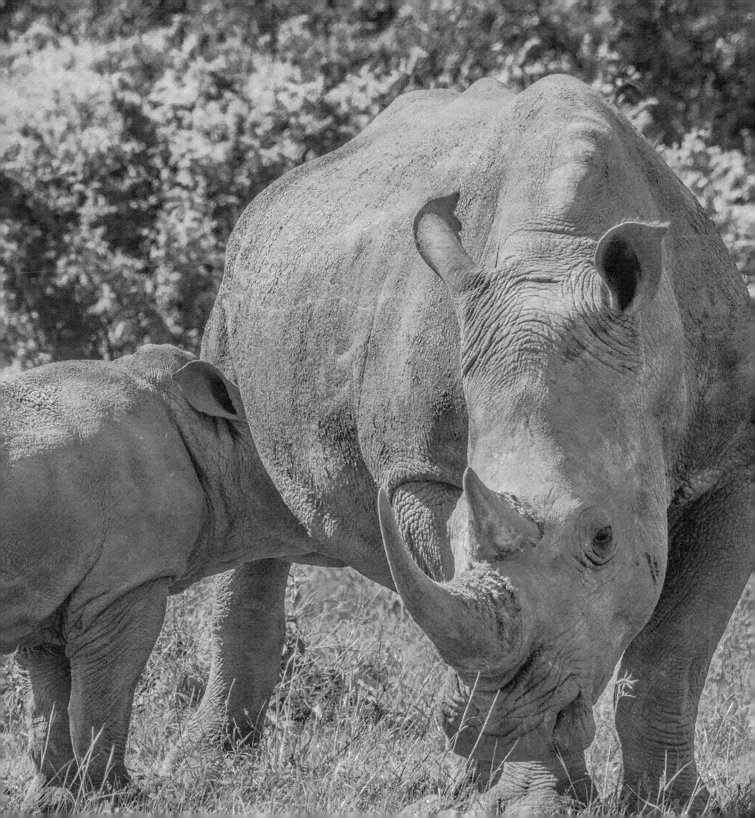

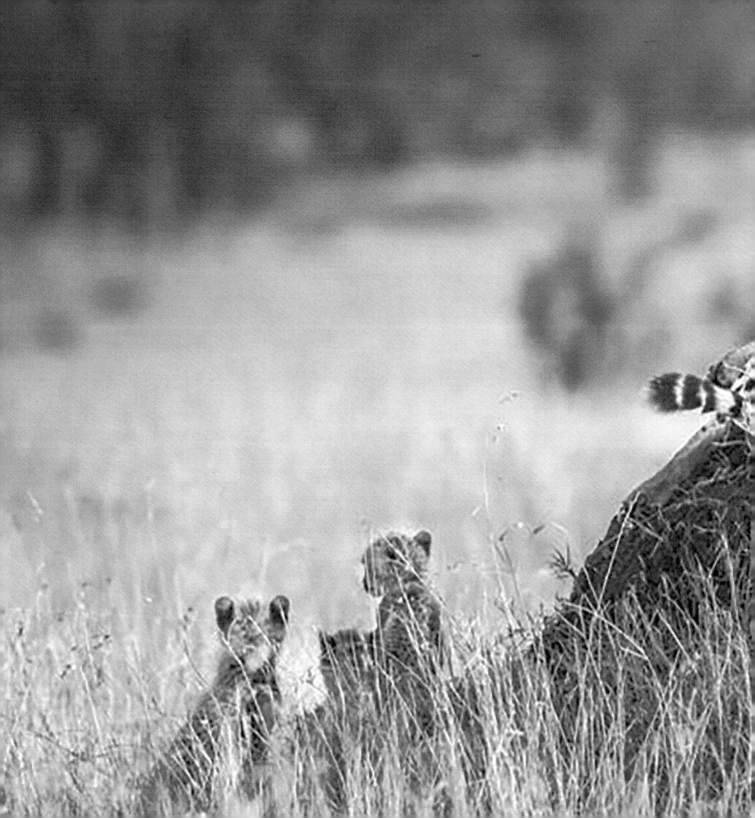

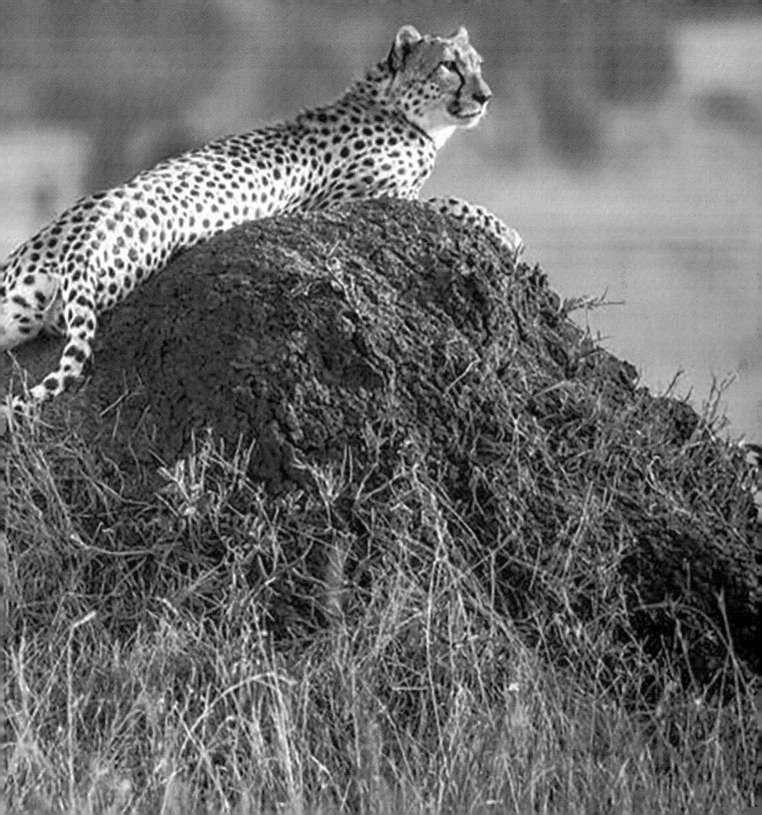

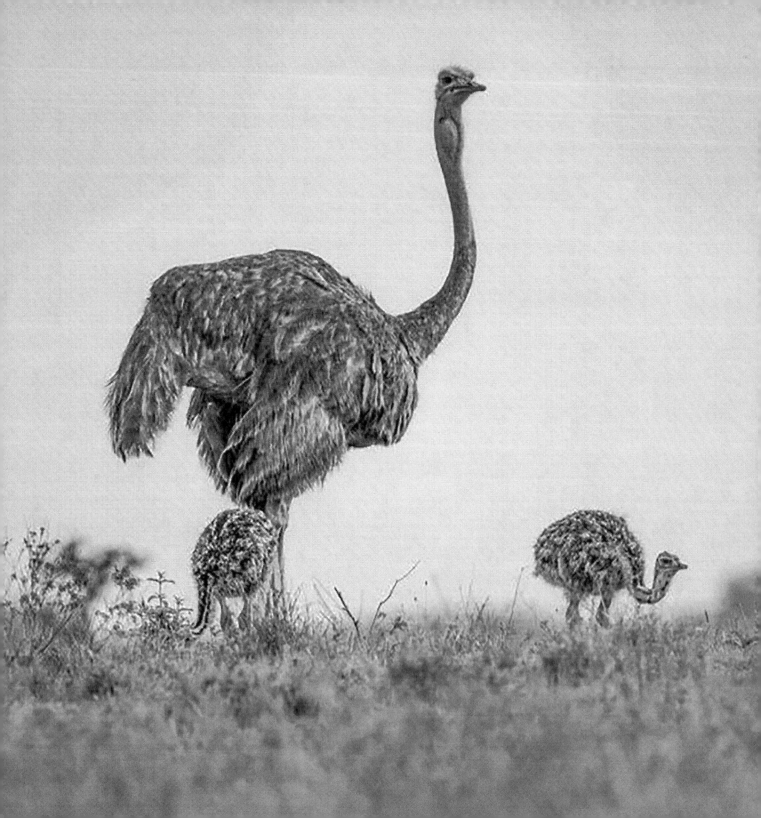

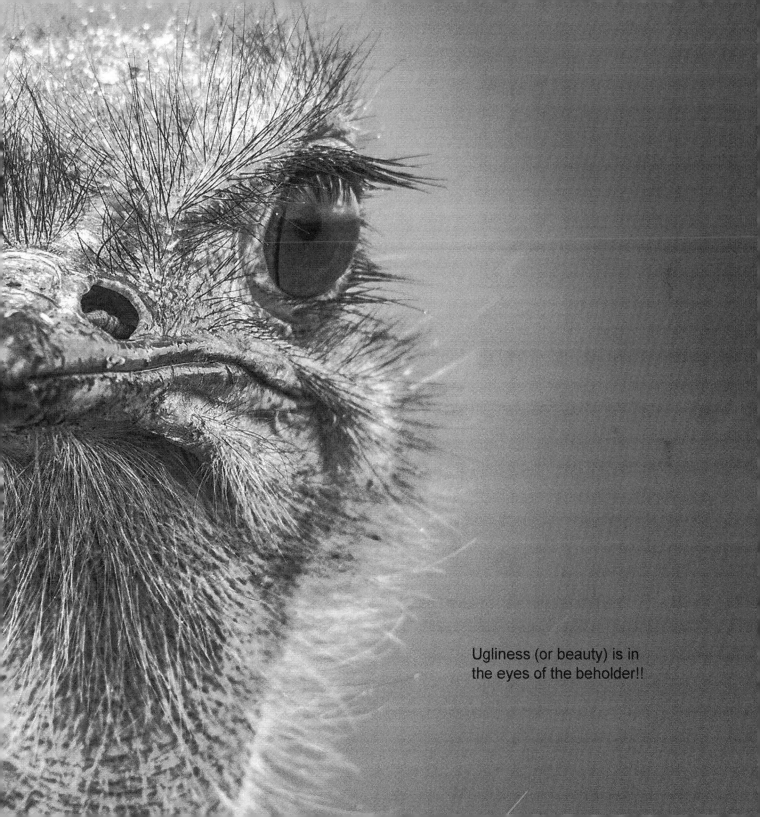

Ugliness (or beauty) is in
the eyes of the beholder!!

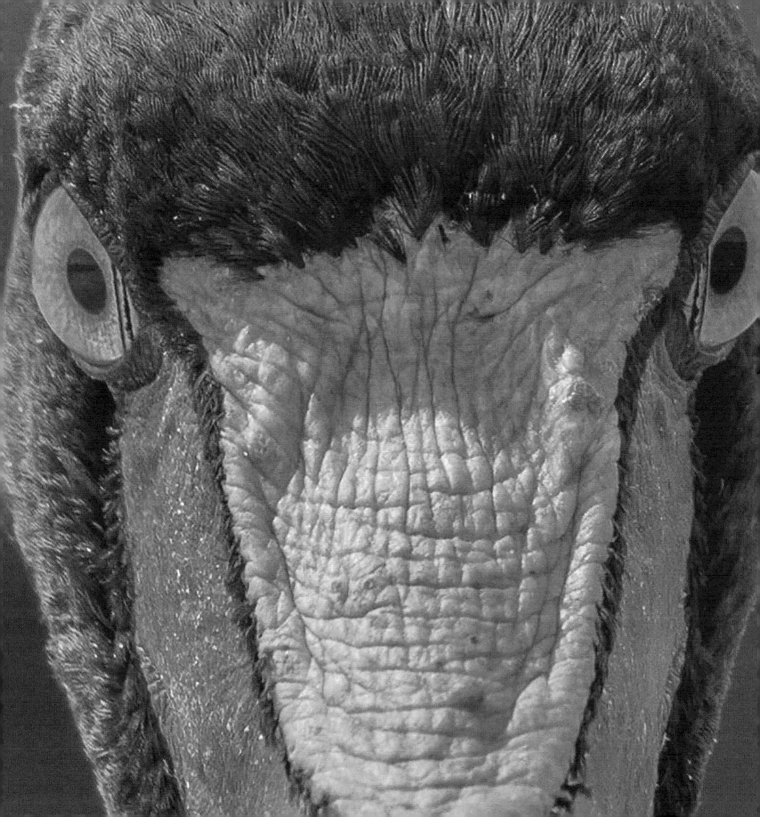

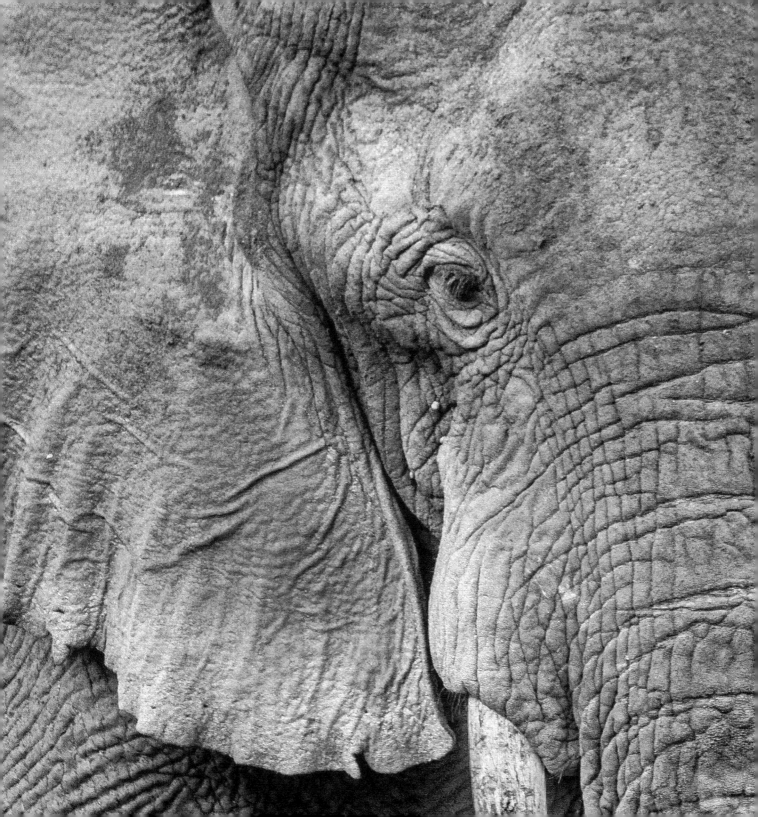

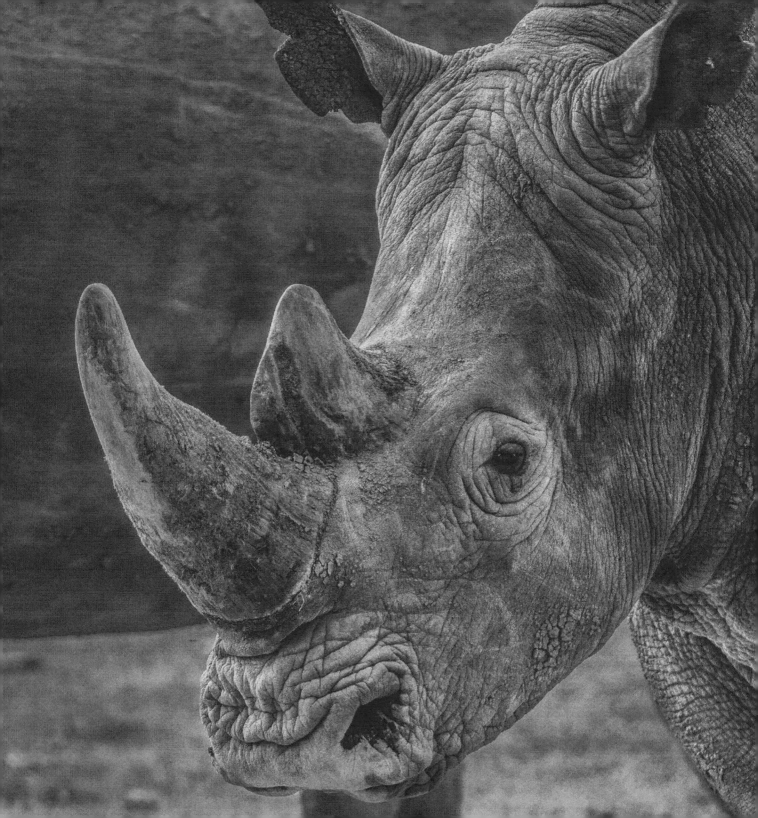

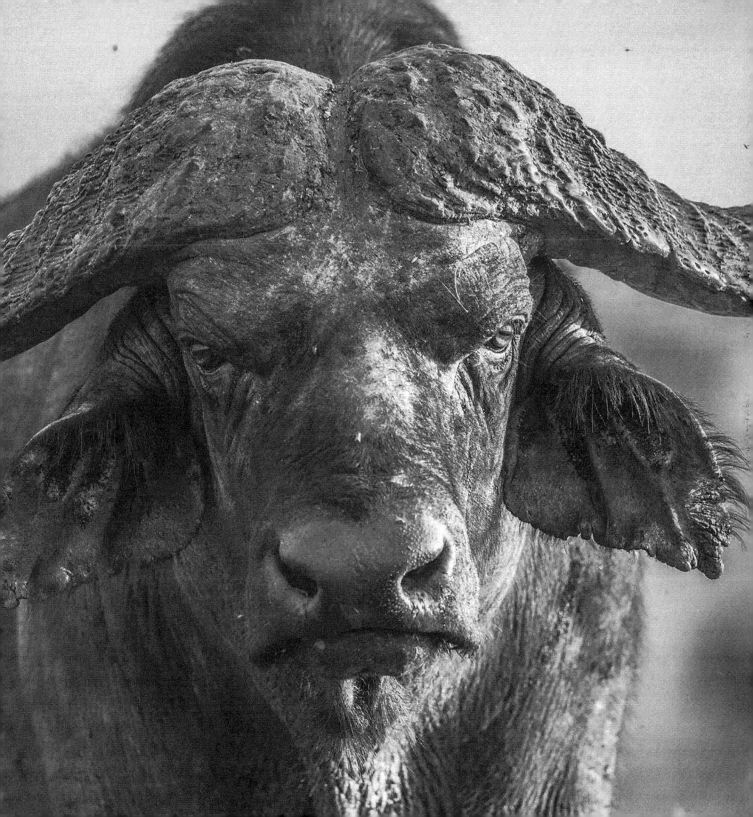

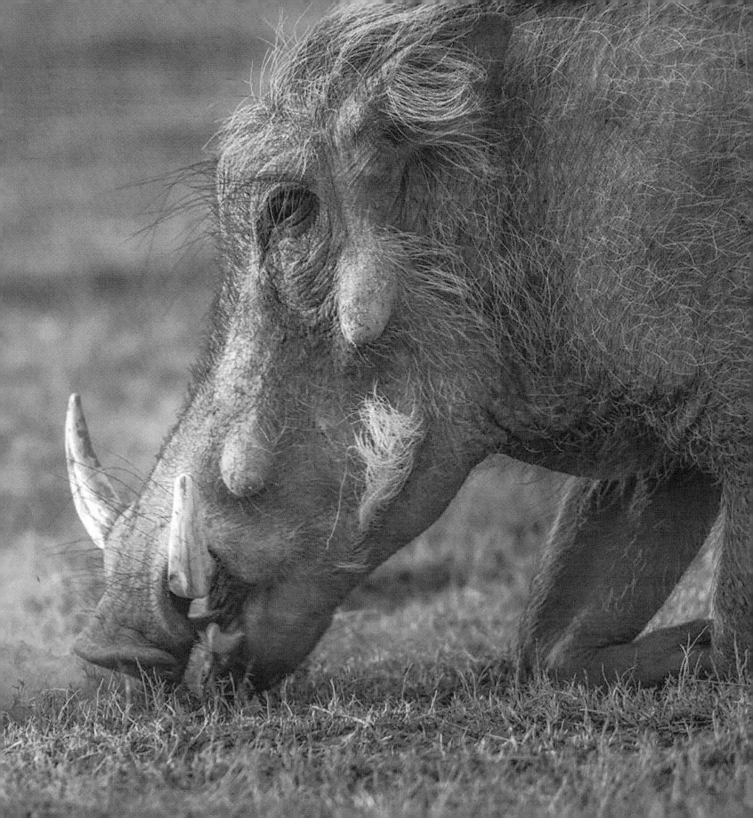

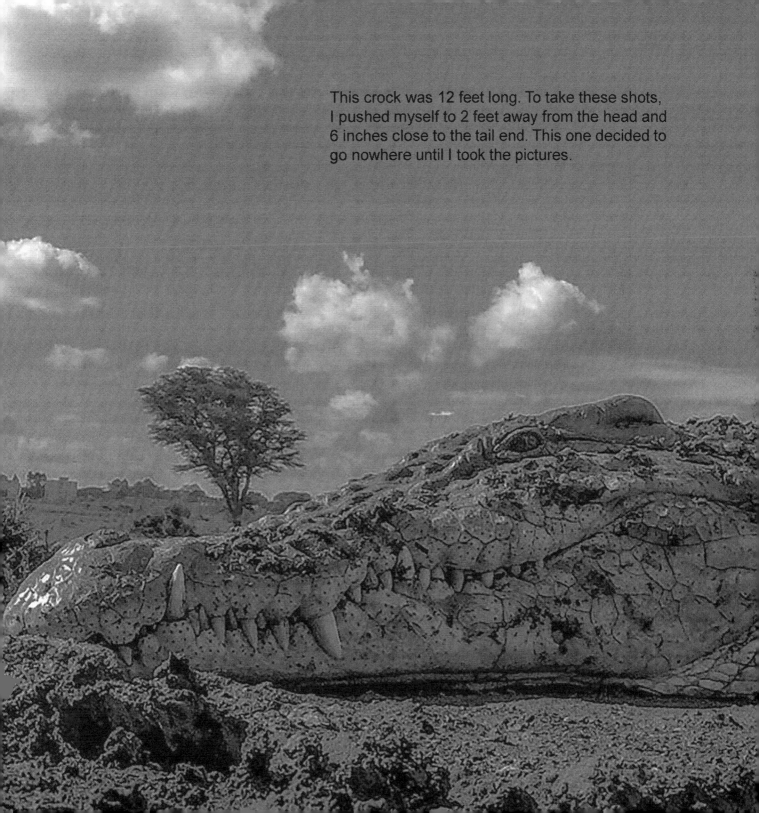

This crock was 12 feet long. To take these shots, I pushed myself to 2 feet away from the head and 6 inches close to the tail end. This one decided to go nowhere until I took the pictures.

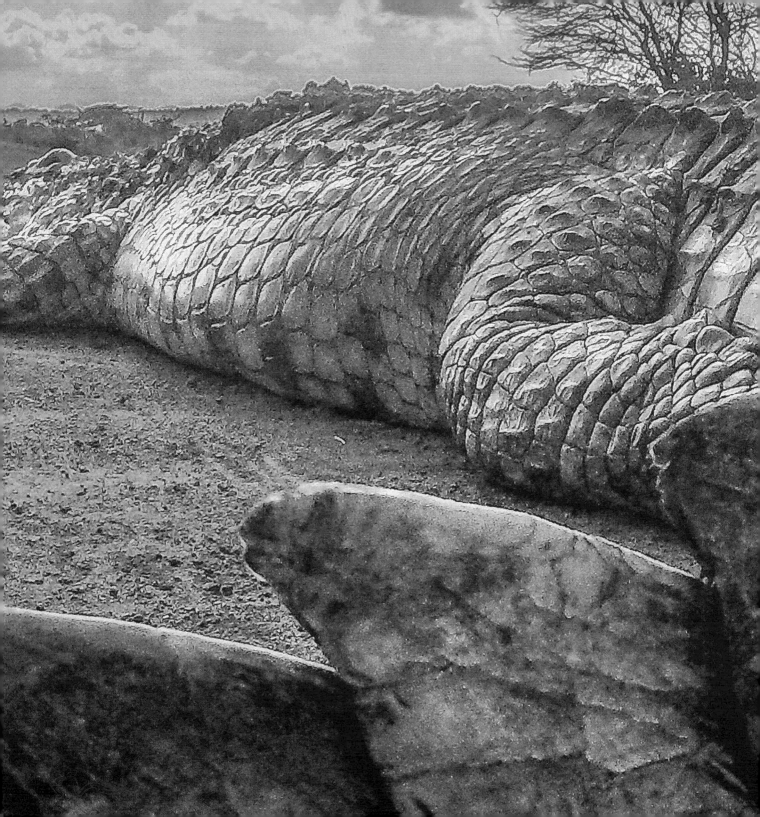

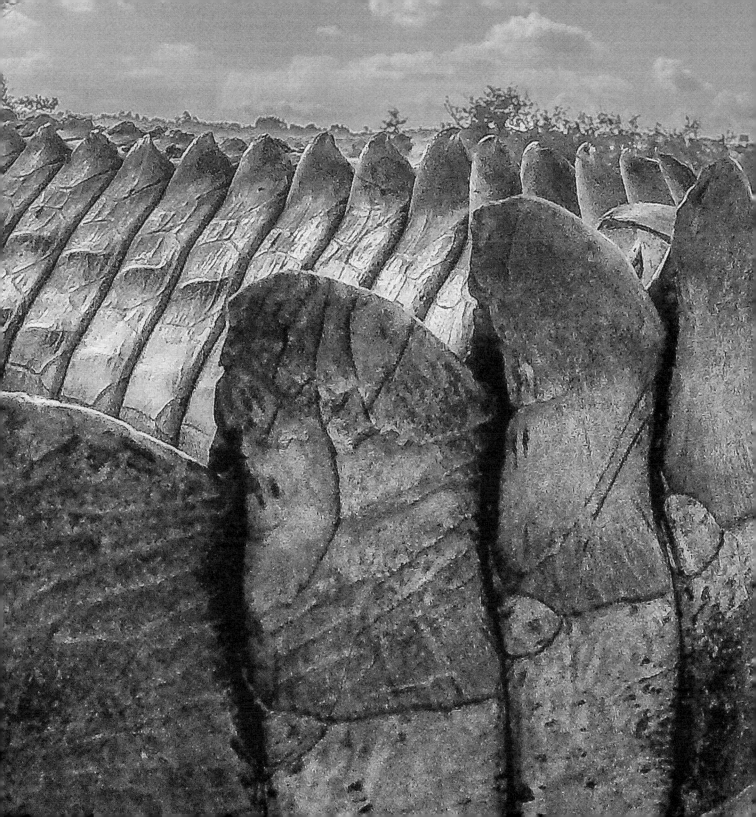

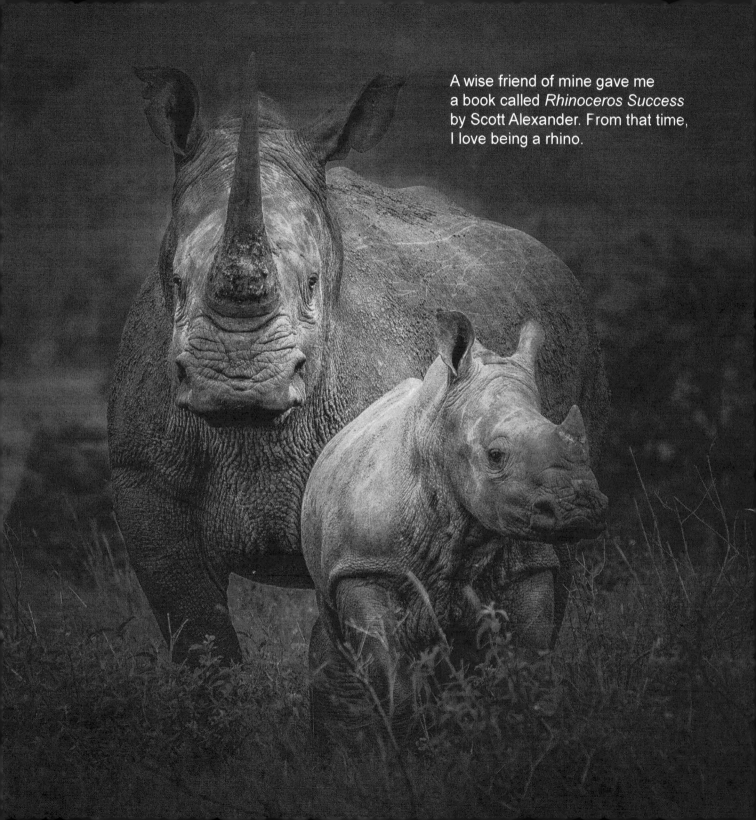

A wise friend of mine gave me
a book called *Rhinoceros Success*
by Scott Alexander. From that time,
I love being a rhino.

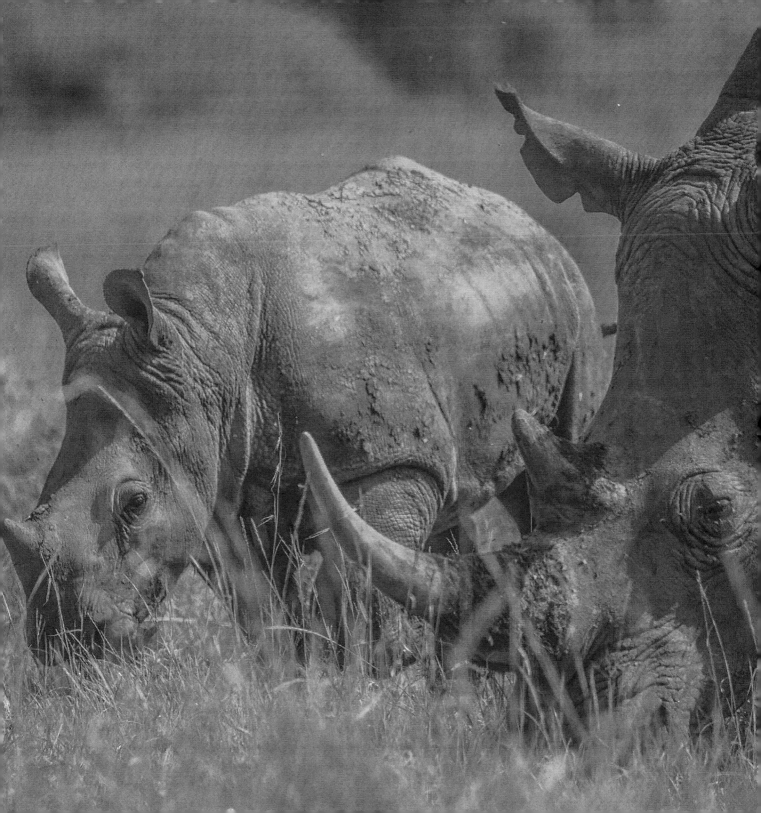

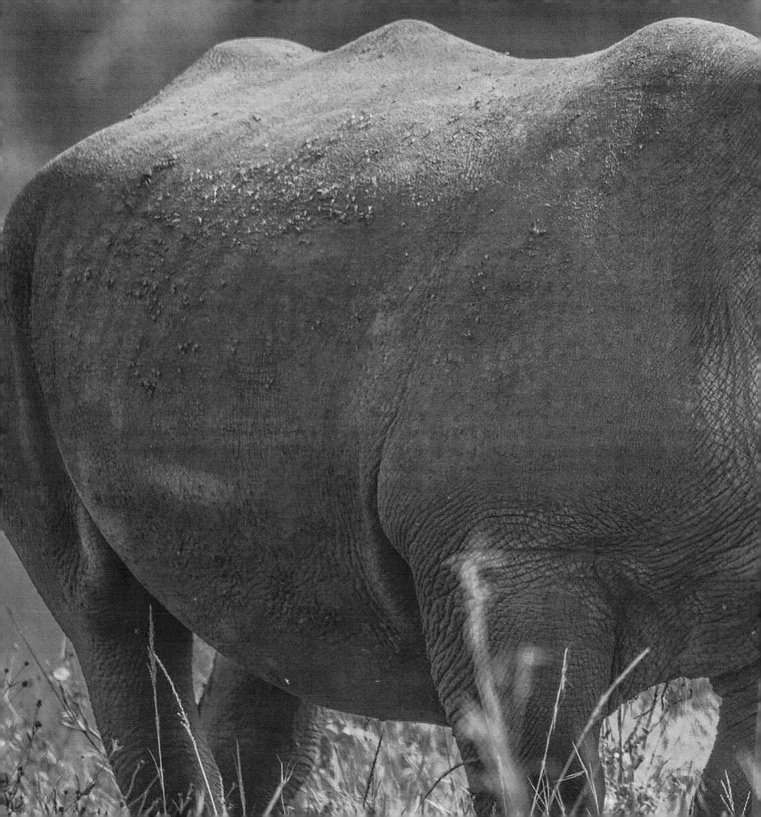

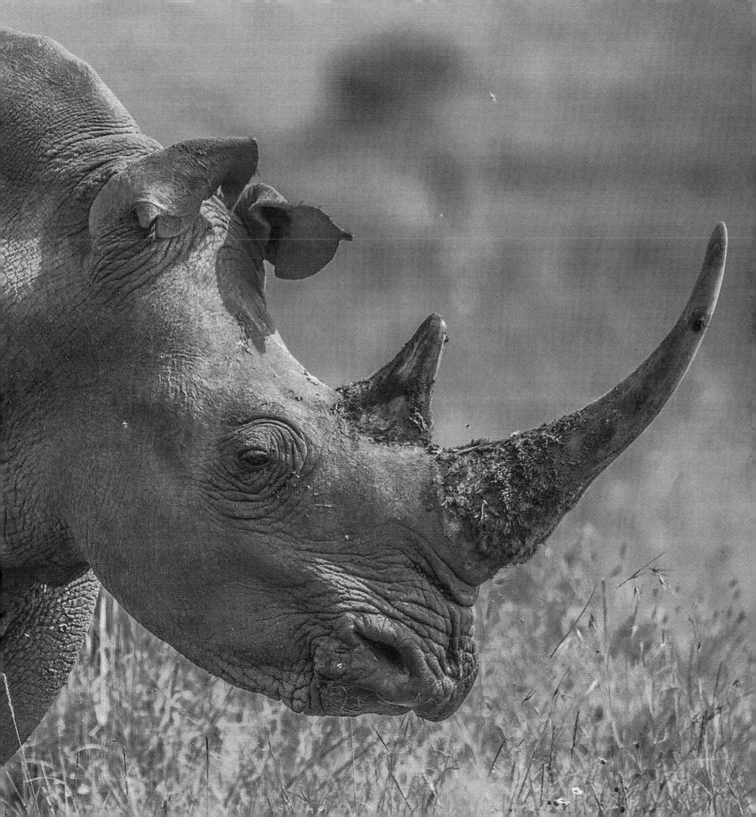

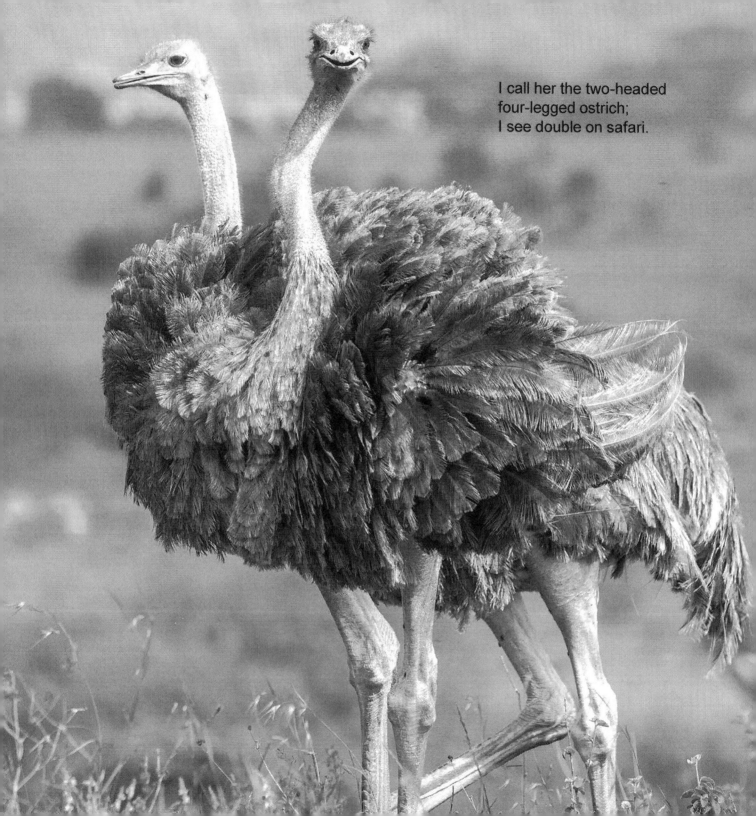

I call her the two-headed
four-legged ostrich;
I see double on safari.

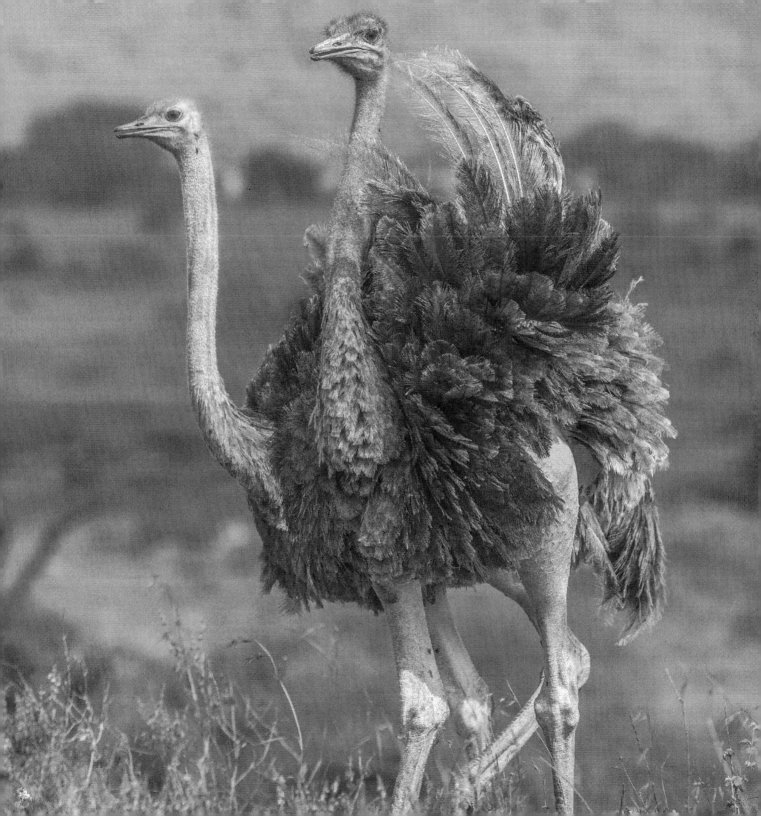

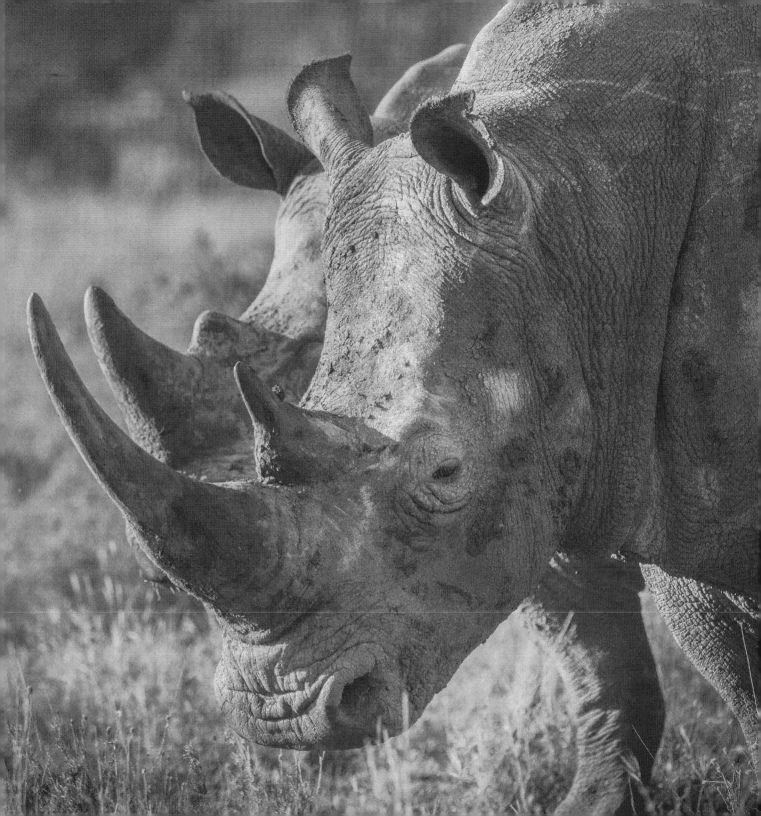

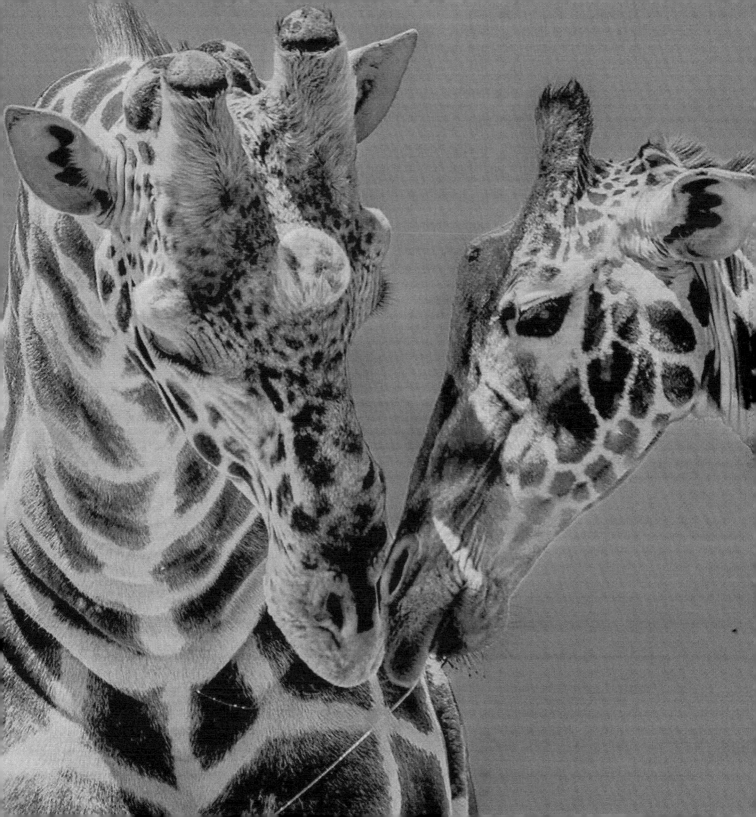

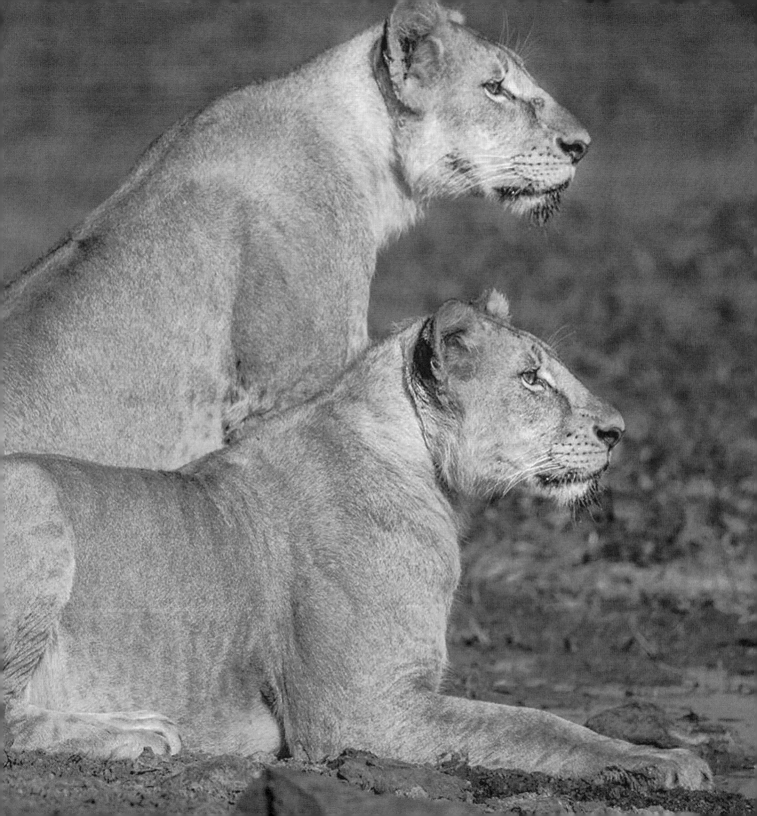

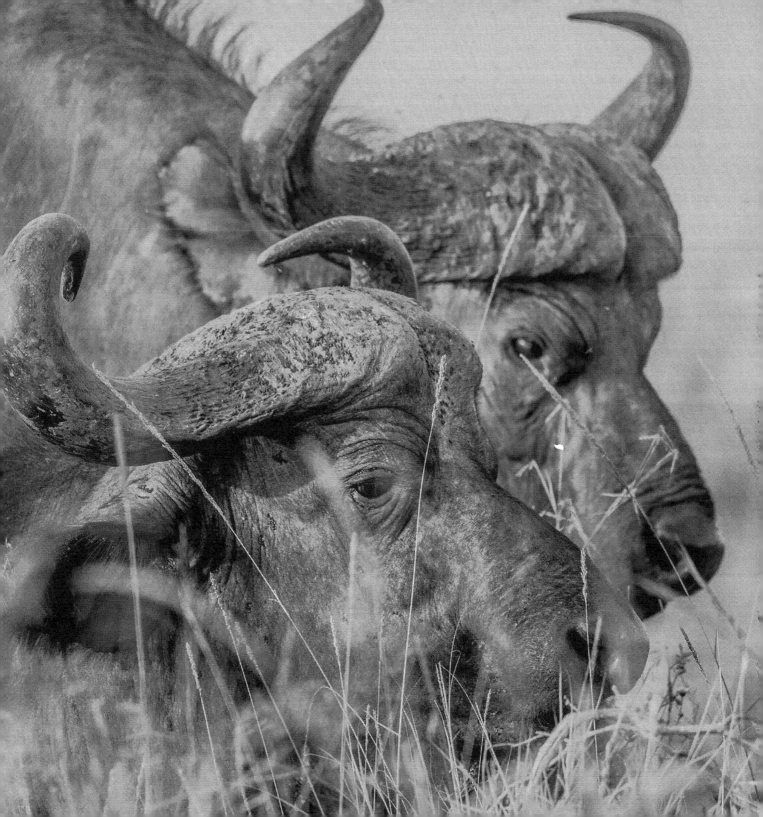

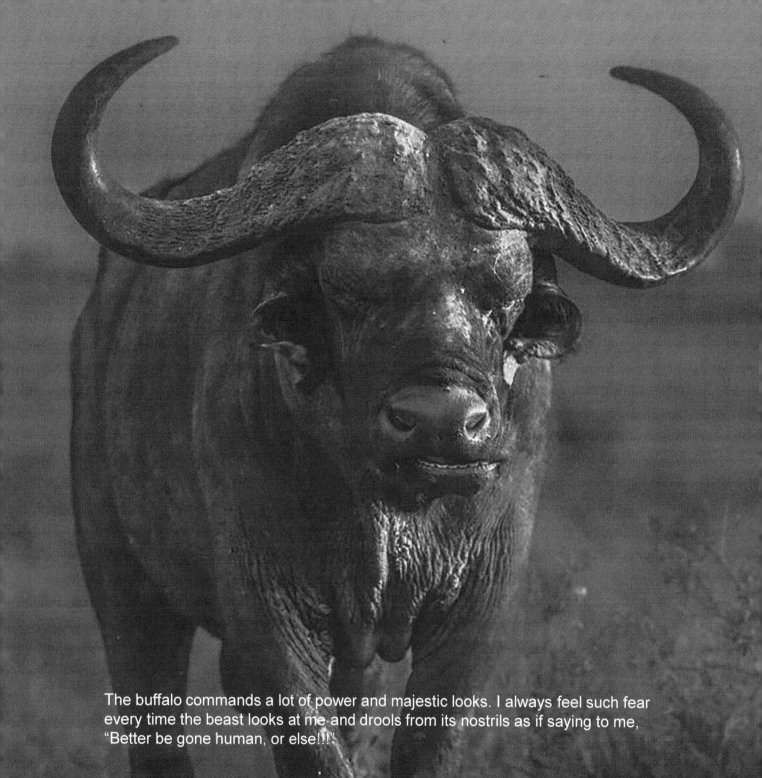

The buffalo commands a lot of power and majestic looks. I always feel such fear every time the beast looks at me and drools from its nostrils as if saying to me, "Better be gone human, or else!!!"

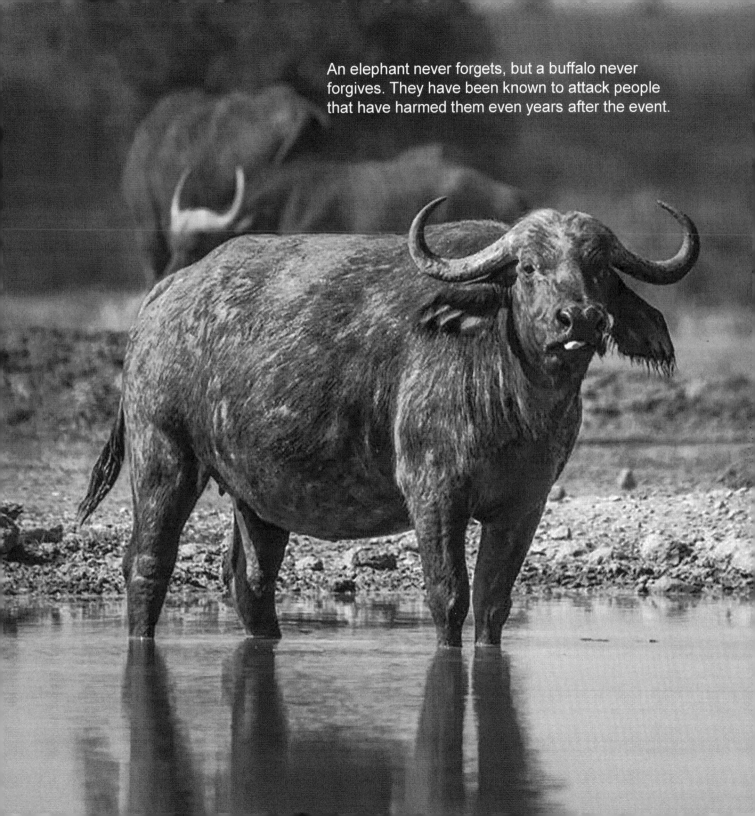

An elephant never forgets, but a buffalo never forgives. They have been known to attack people that have harmed them even years after the event.

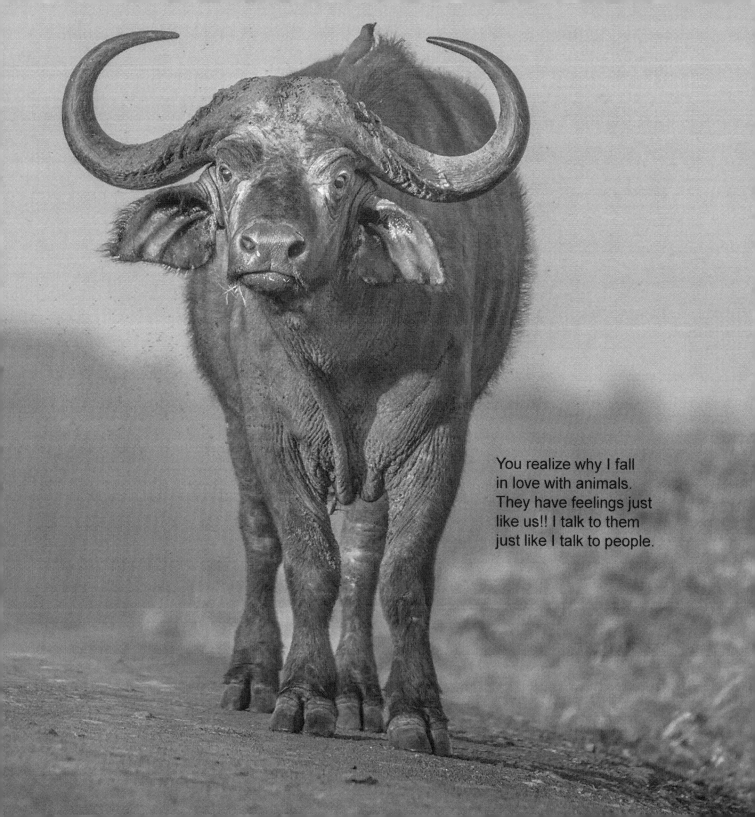

You realize why I fall
in love with animals.
They have feelings just
like us!! I talk to them
just like I talk to people.

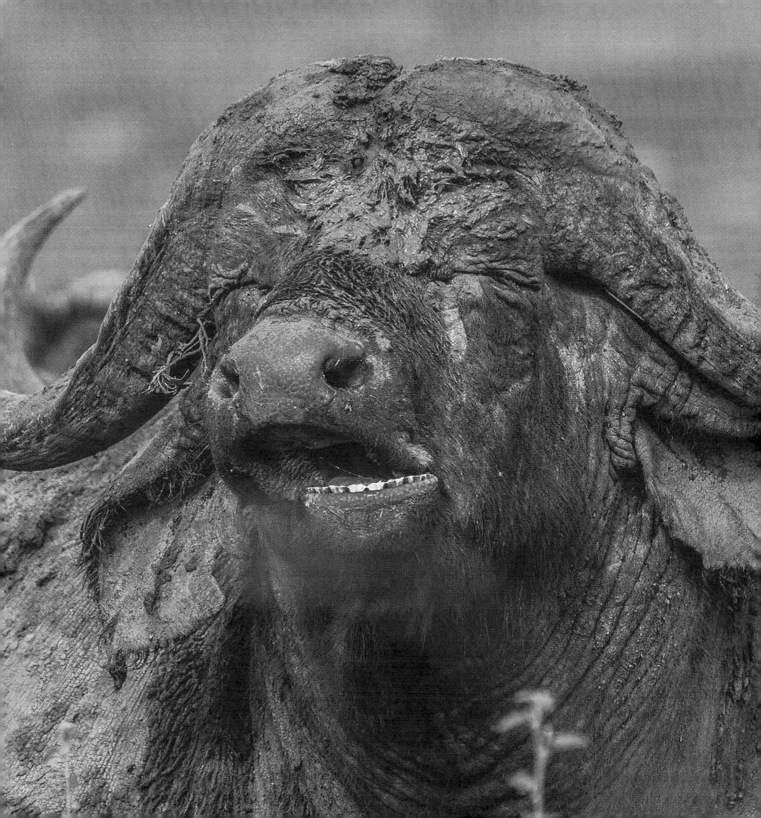

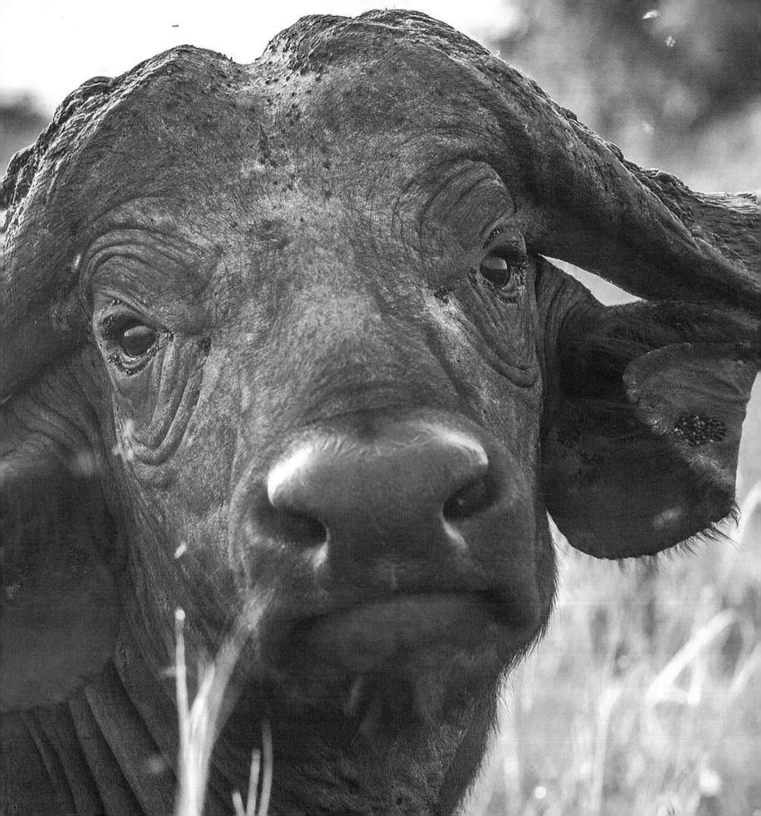

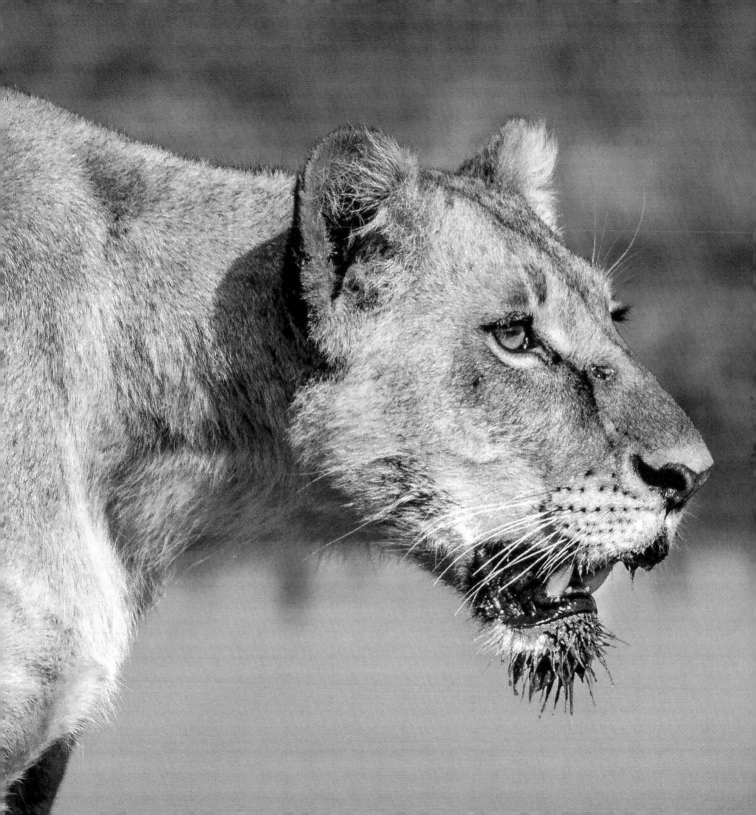

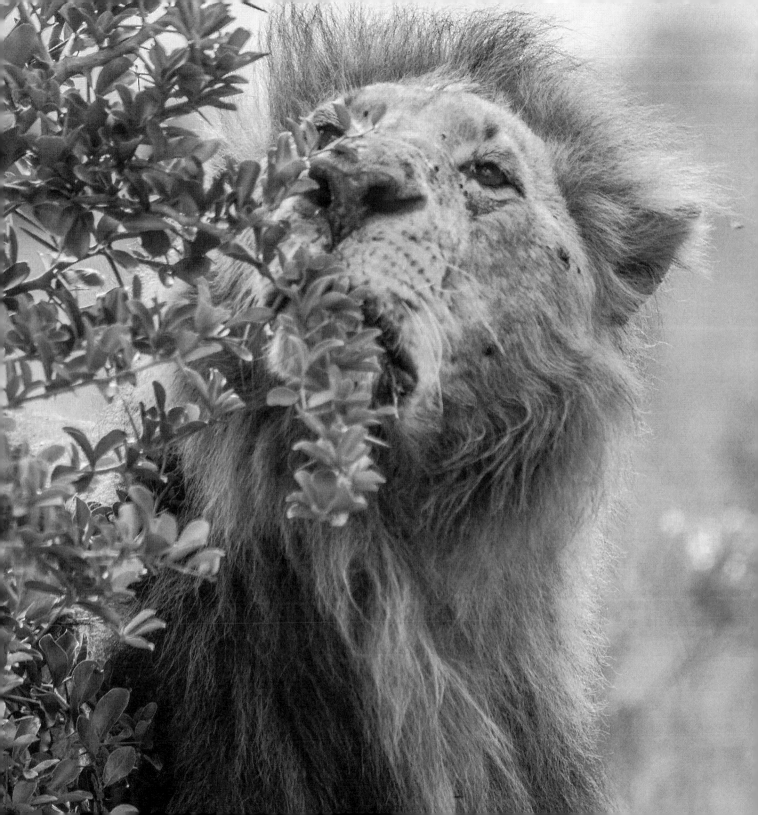

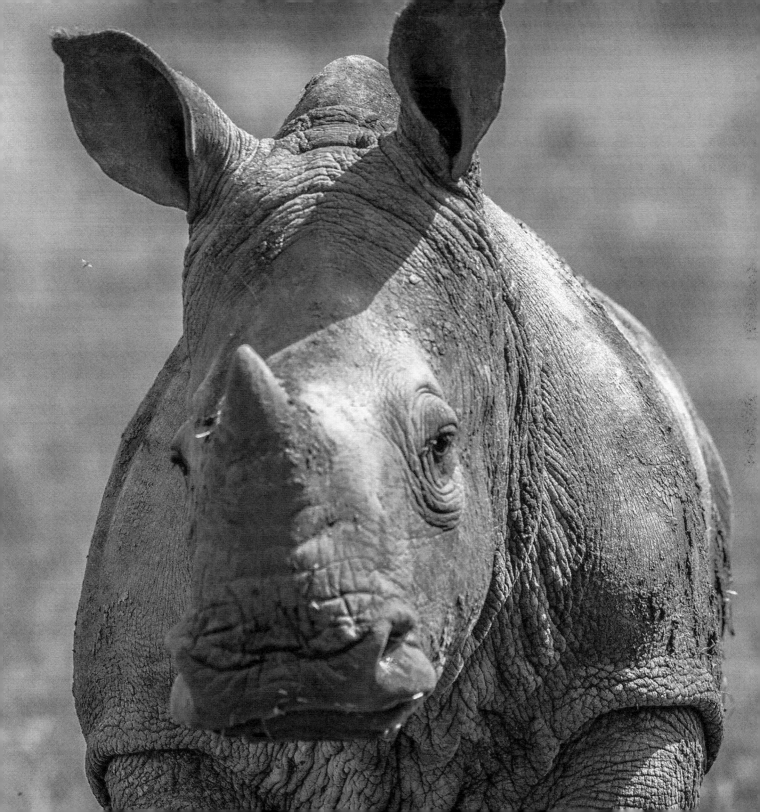

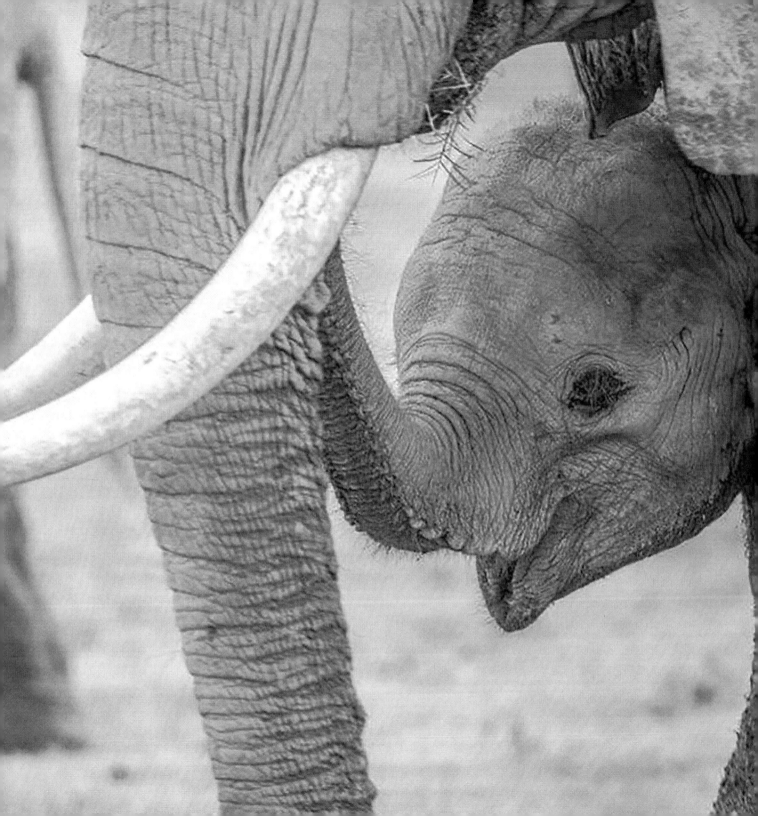

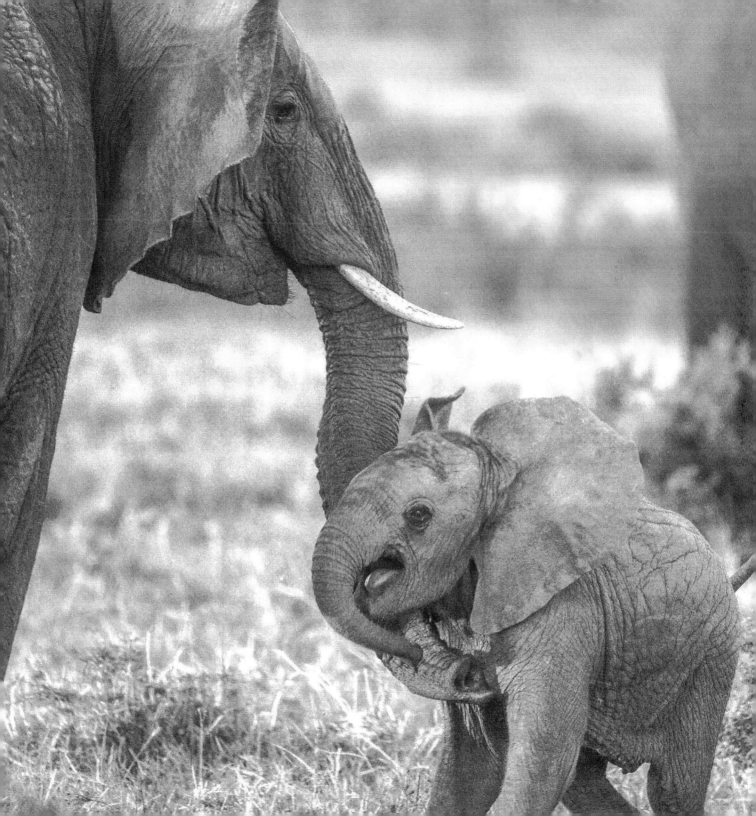

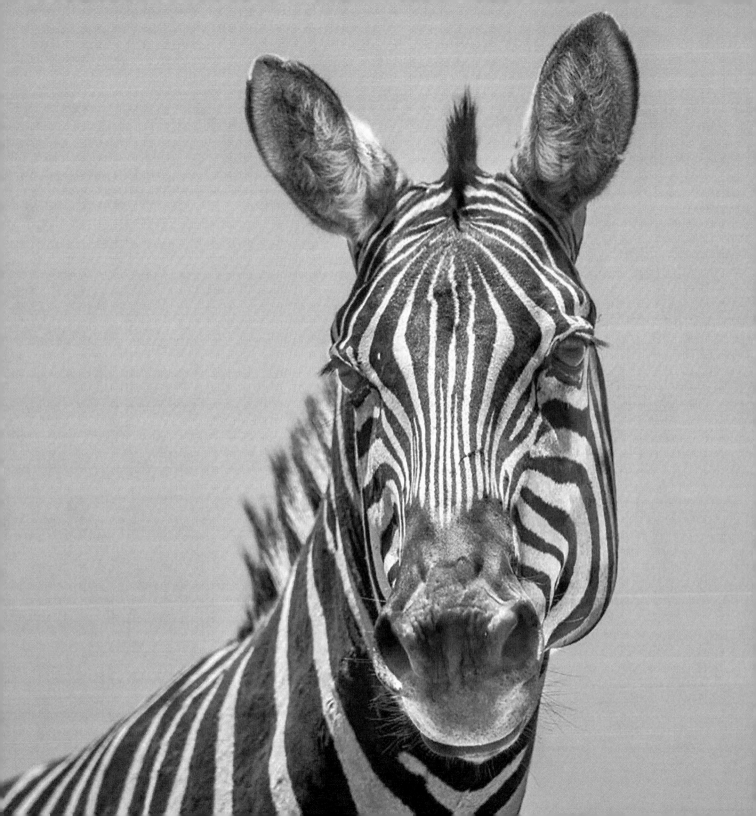

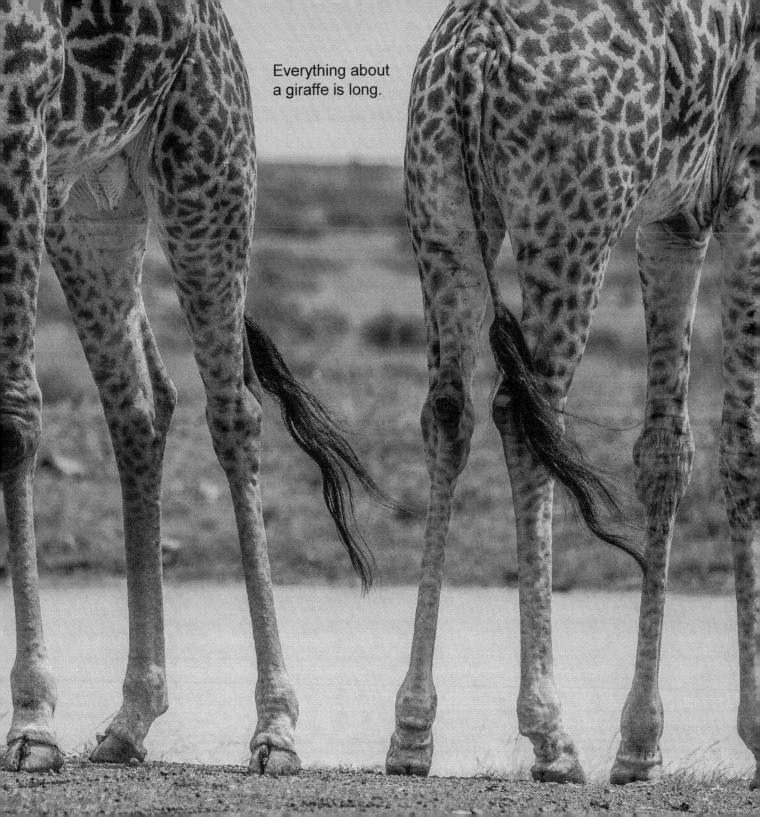

Everything about
a giraffe is long.

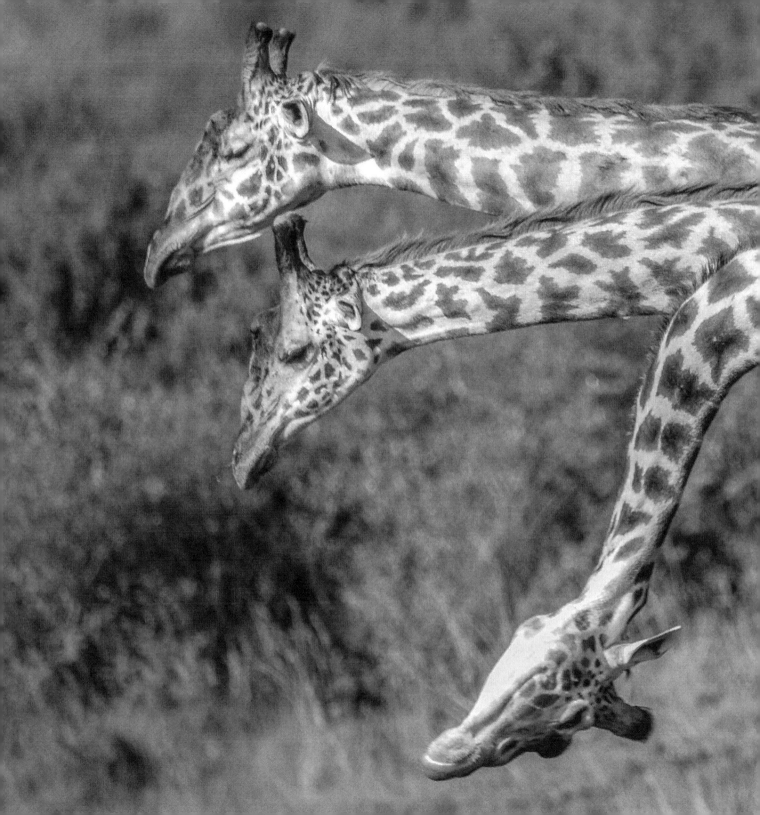

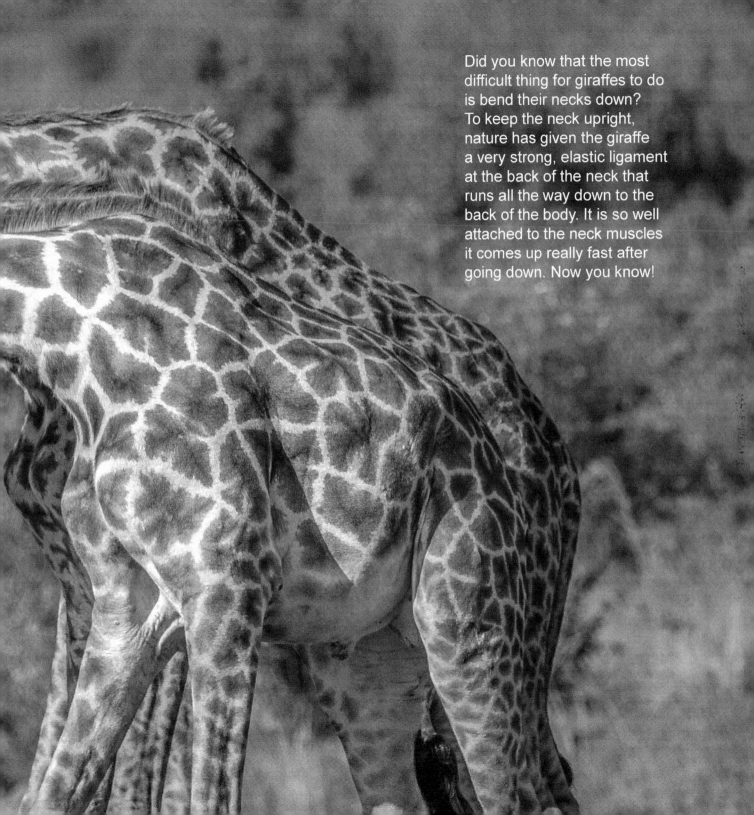

Did you know that the most difficult thing for giraffes to do is bend their necks down? To keep the neck upright, nature has given the giraffe a very strong, elastic ligament at the back of the neck that runs all the way down to the back of the body. It is so well attached to the neck muscles it comes up really fast after going down. Now you know!

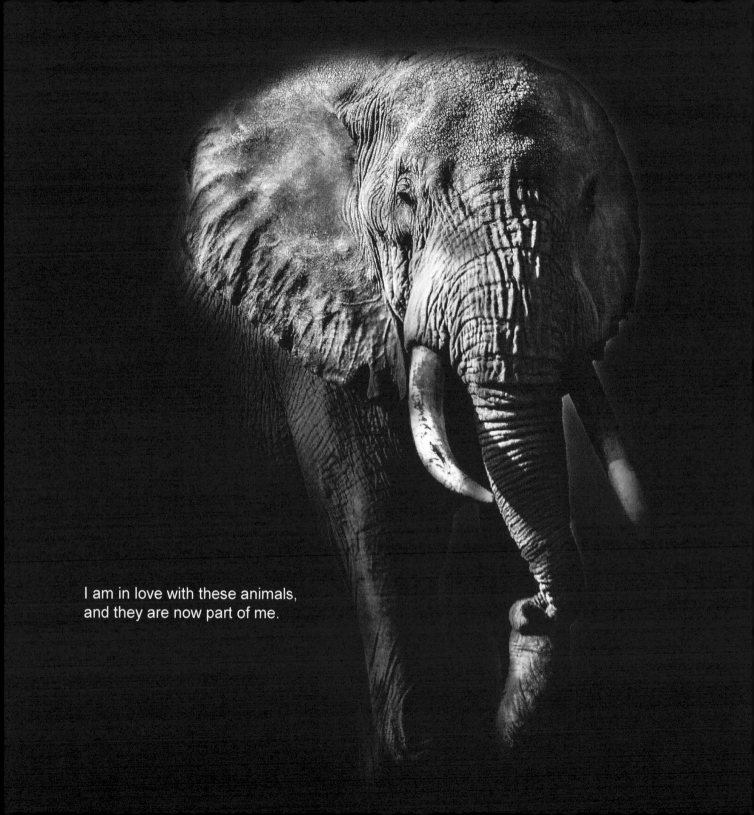

I am in love with these animals,
and they are now part of me.

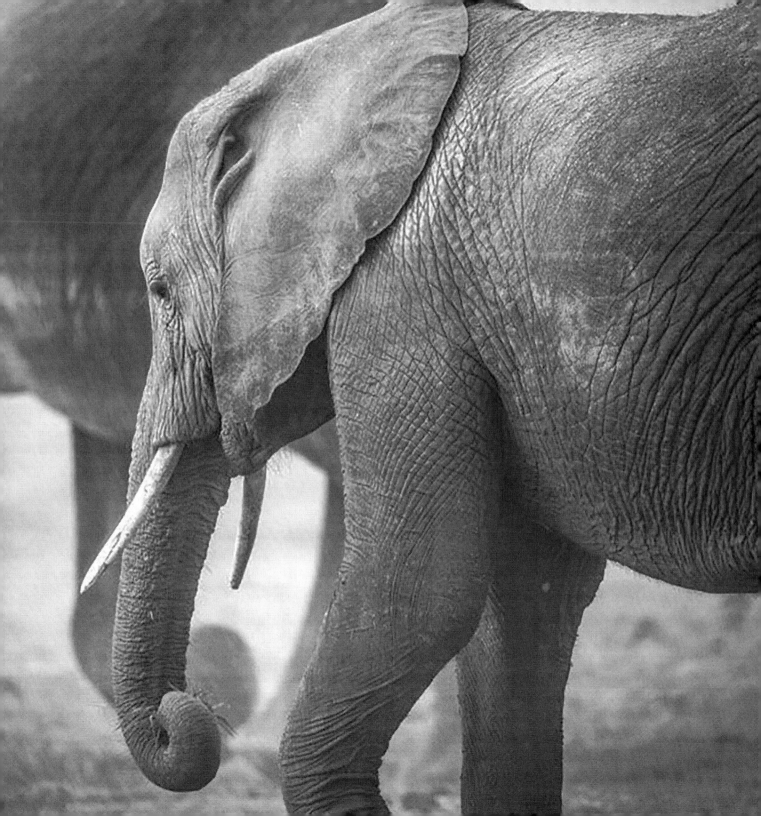

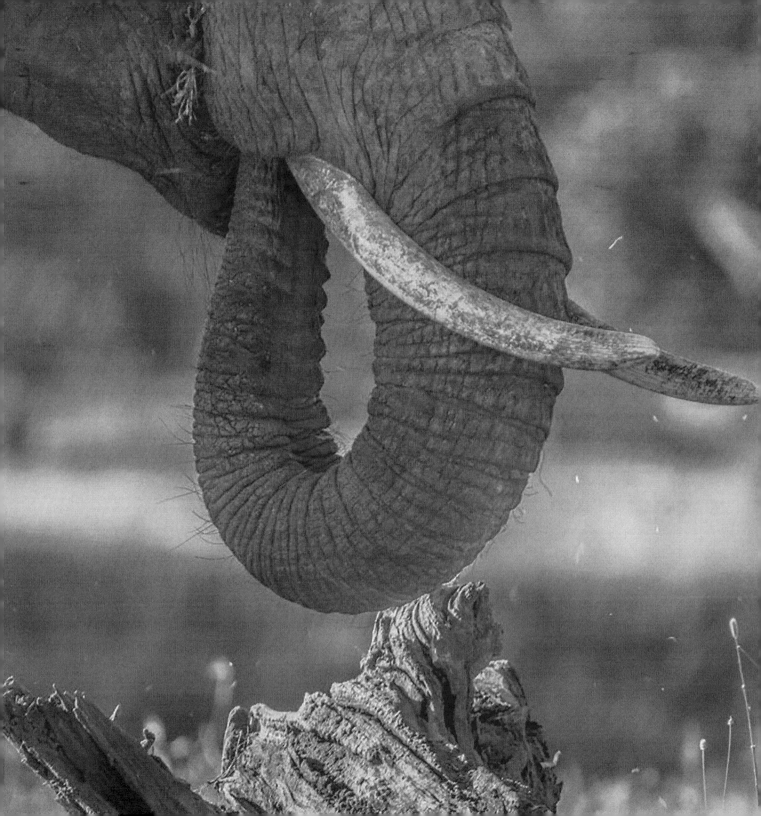

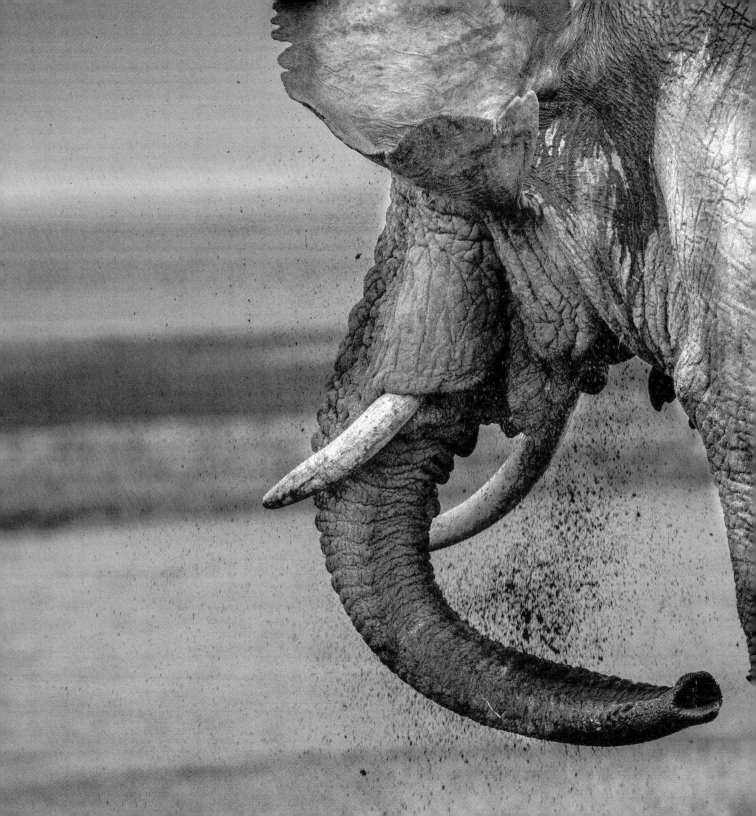

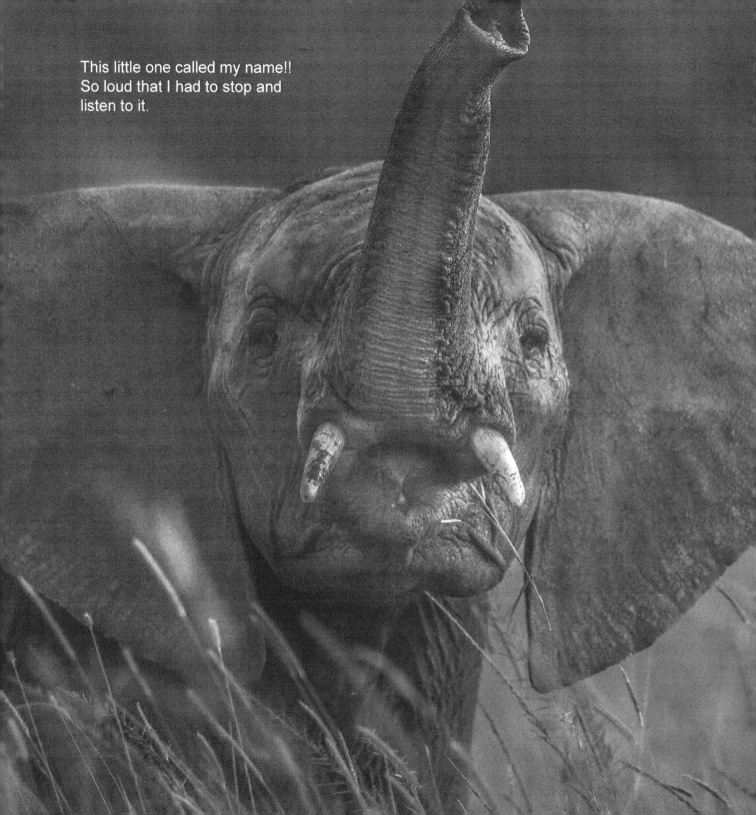

This little one called my name!!
So loud that I had to stop and
listen to it.

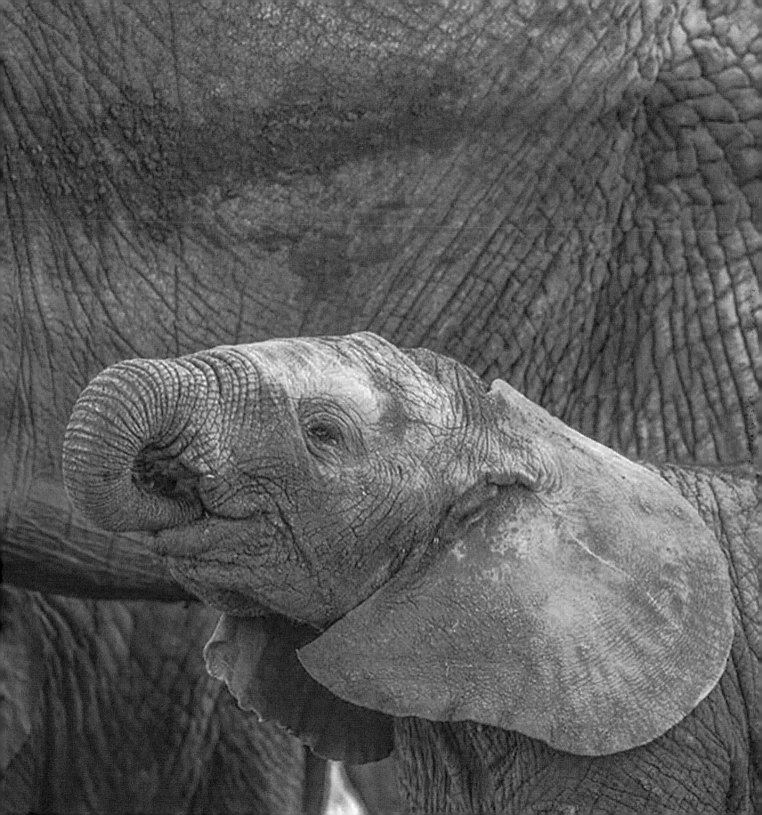

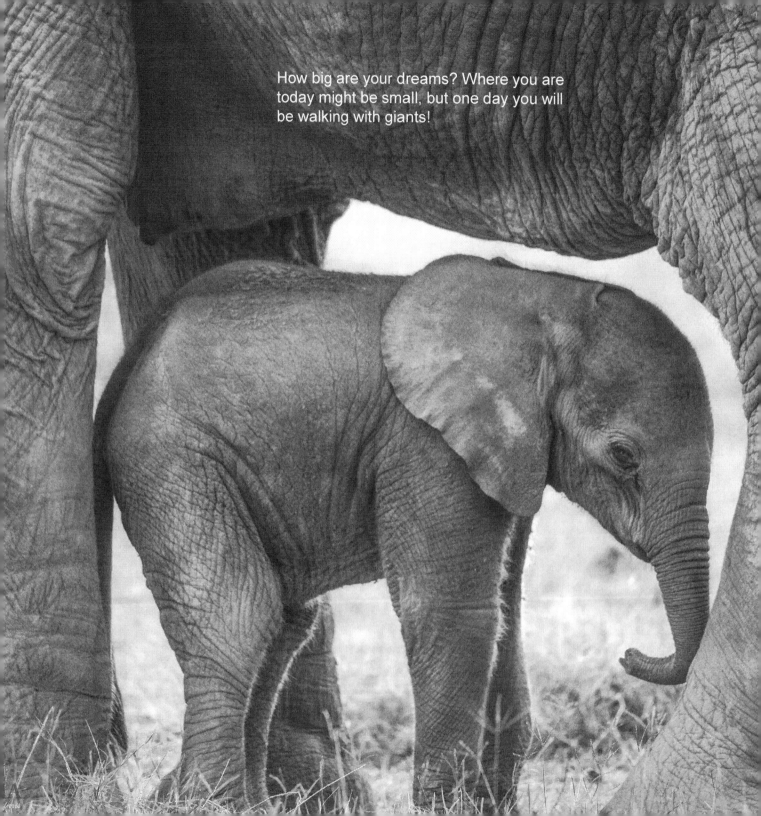

How big are your dreams? Where you are today might be small, but one day you will be walking with giants!

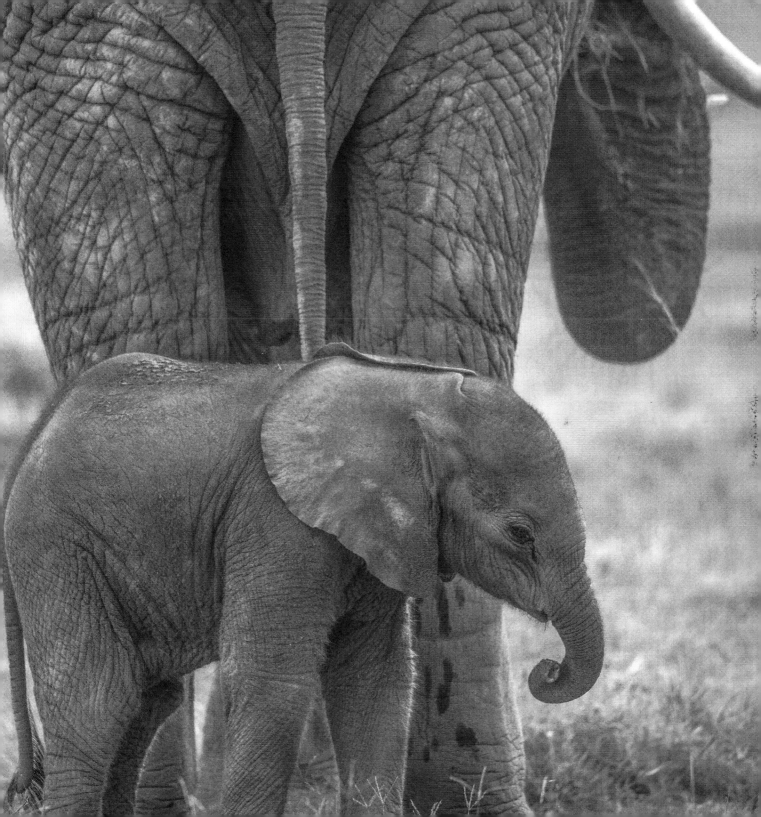

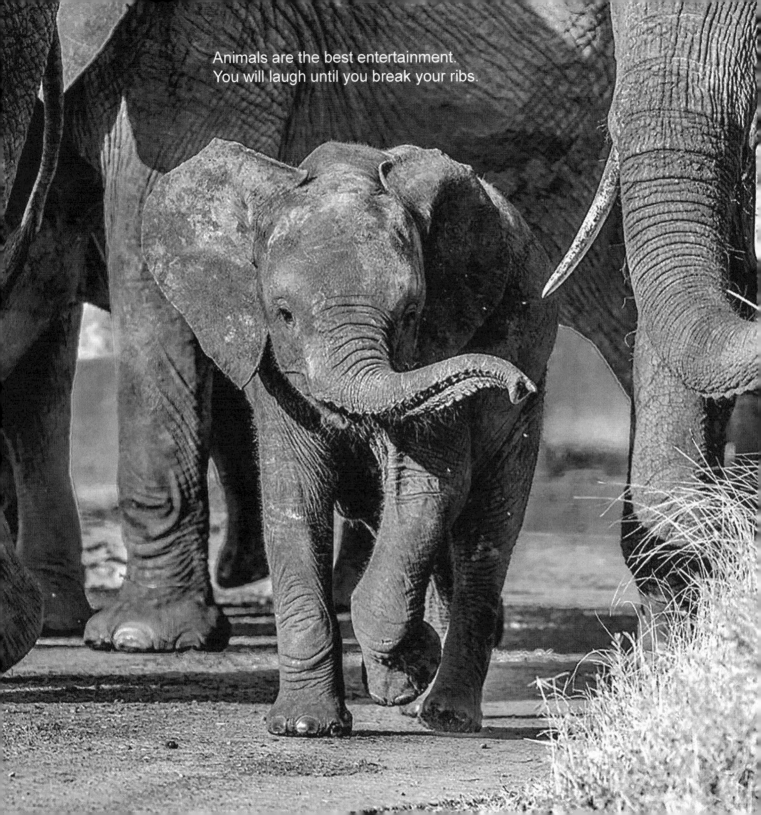

Animals are the best entertainment.
You will laugh until you break your ribs.

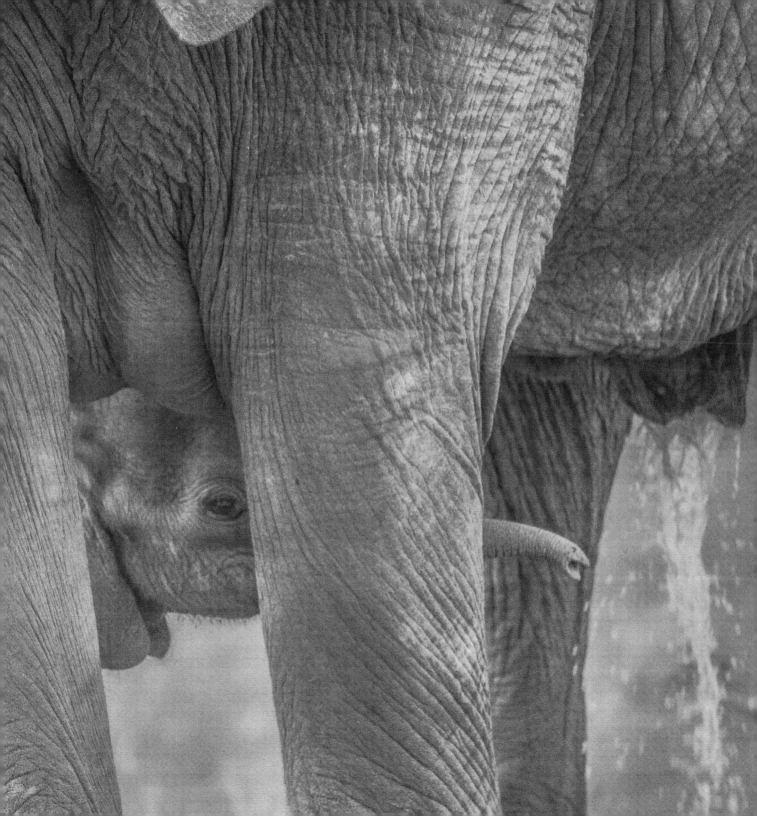

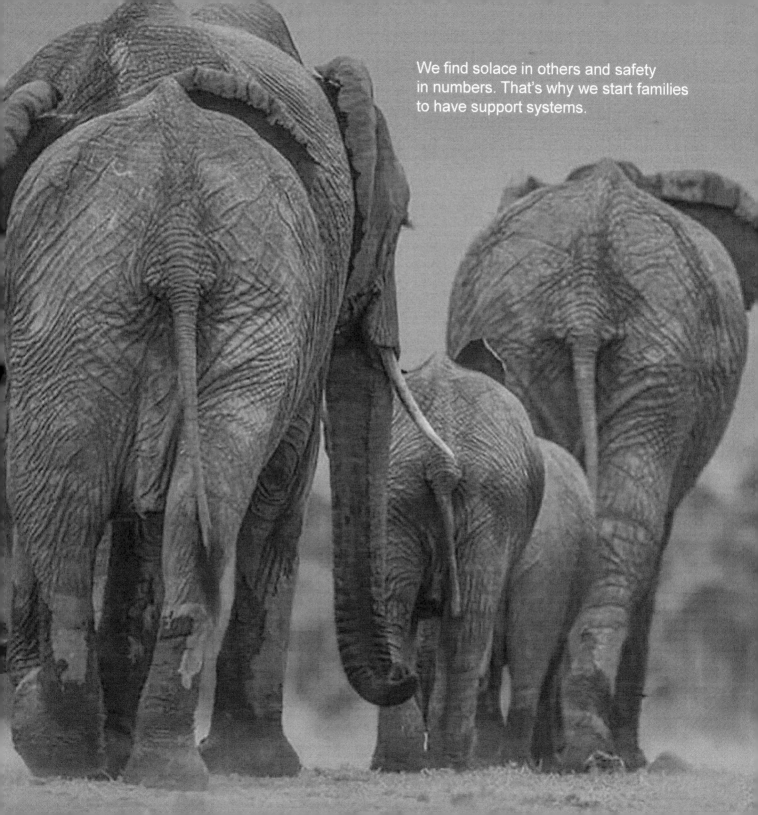

We find solace in others and safety in numbers. That's why we start families to have support systems.

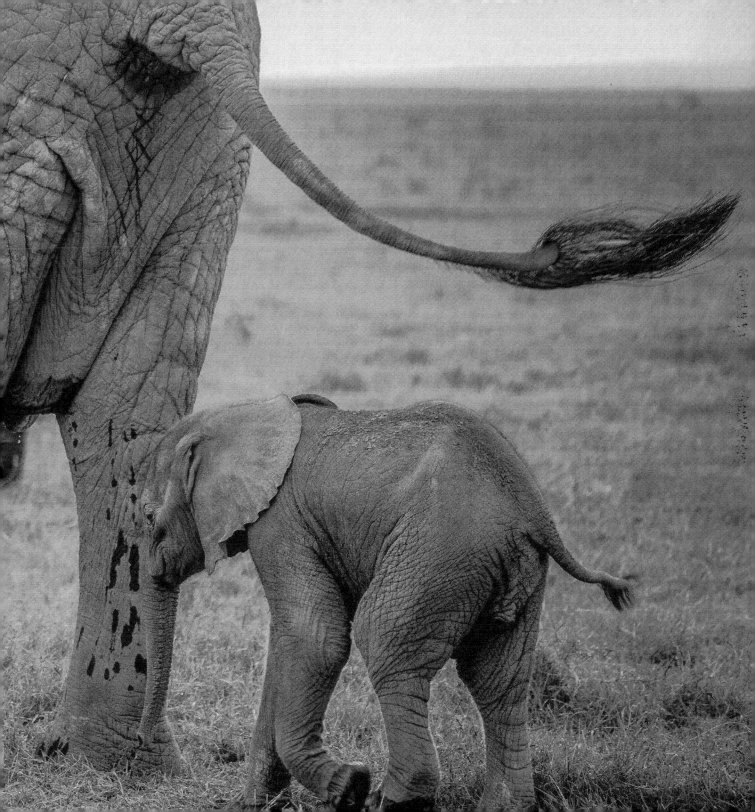

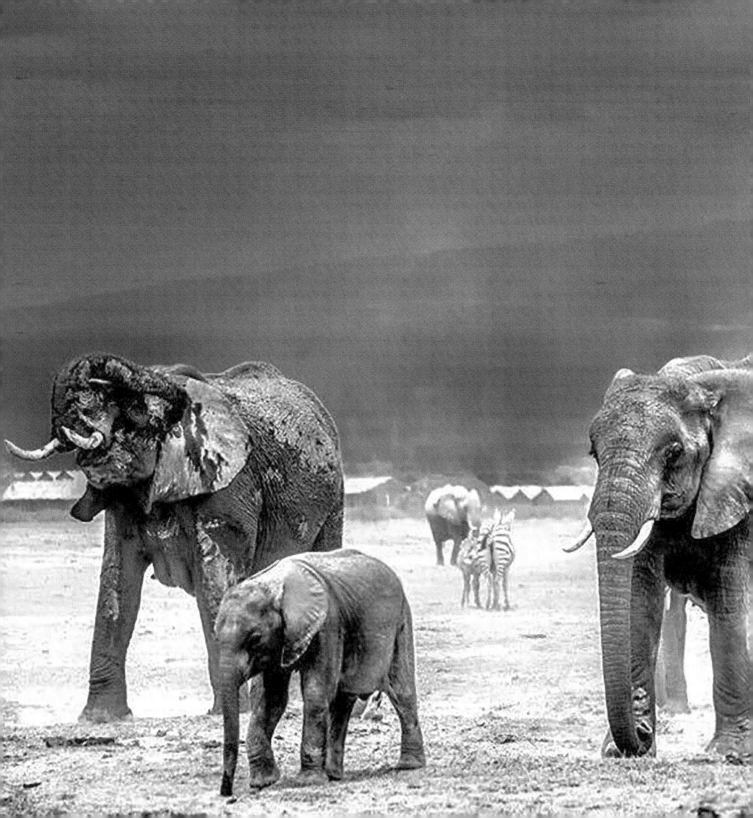

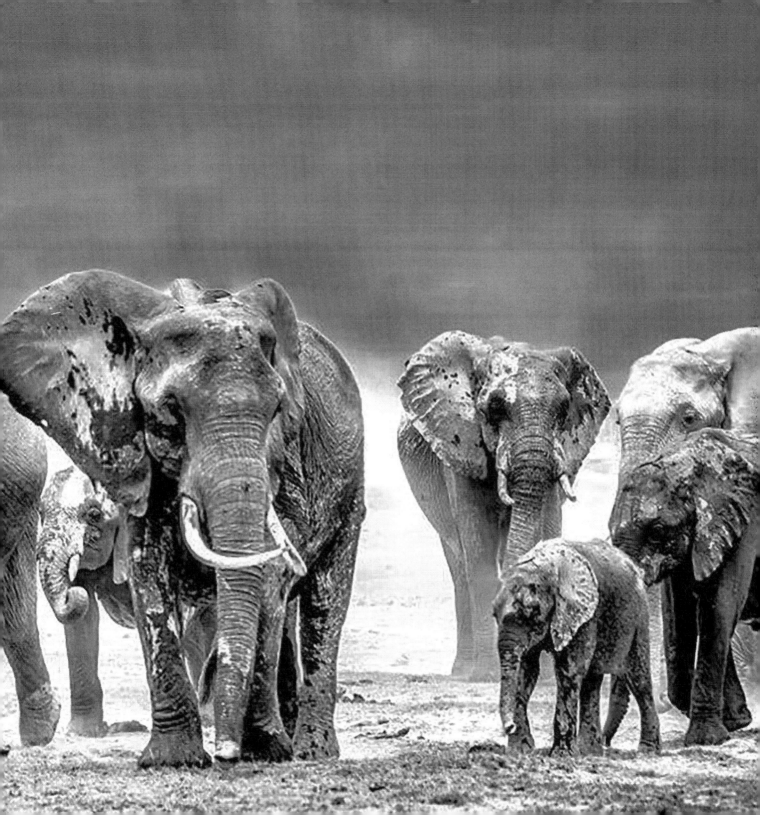

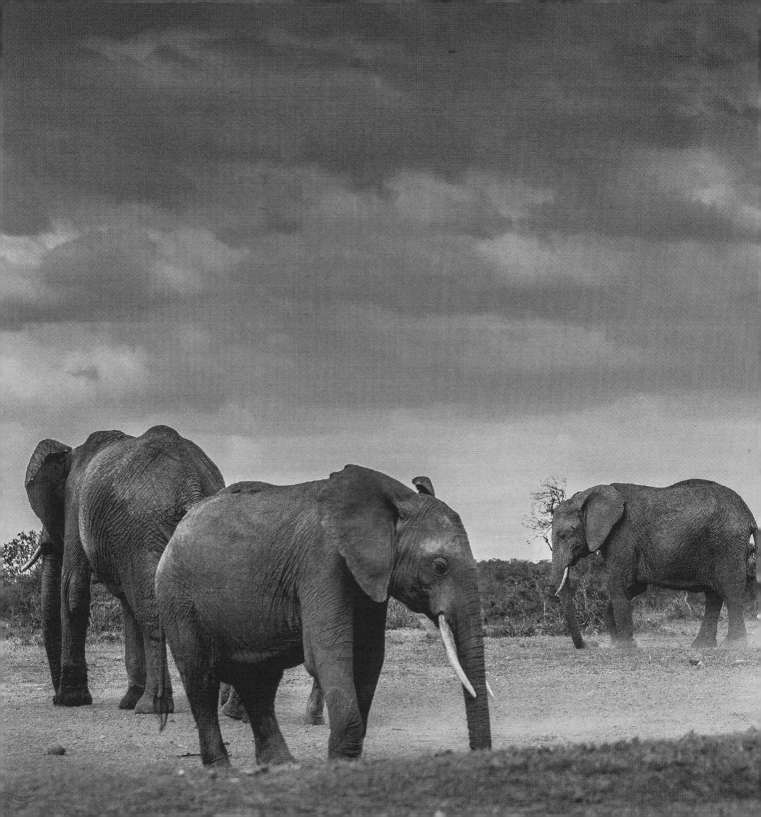

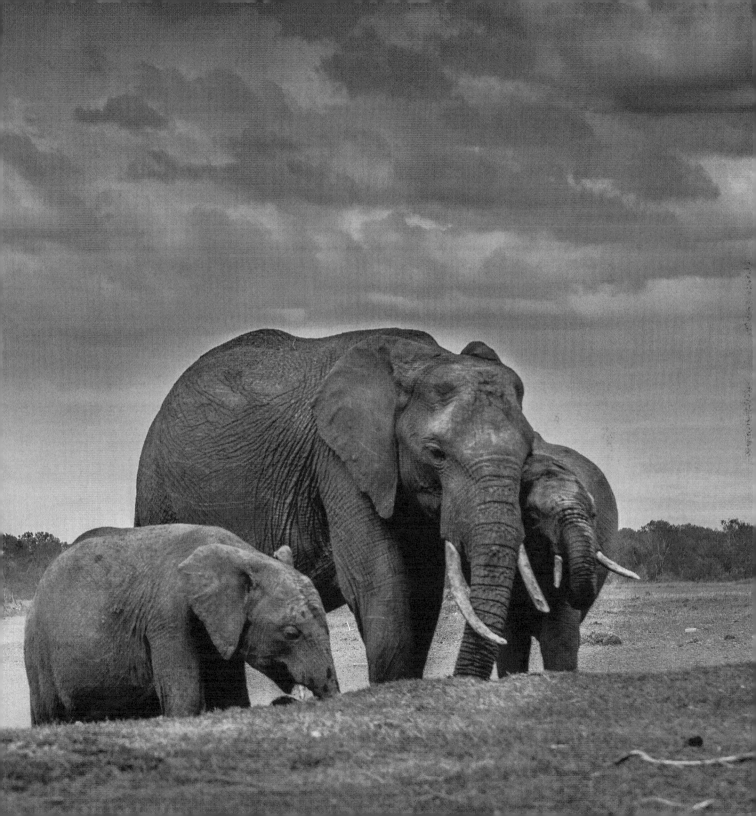

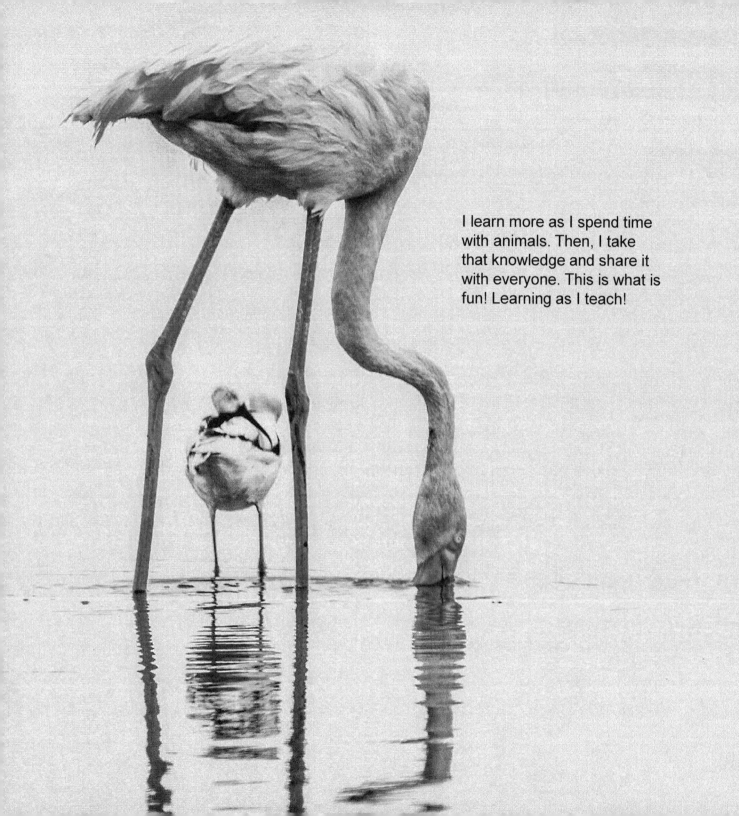

I learn more as I spend time with animals. Then, I take that knowledge and share it with everyone. This is what is fun! Learning as I teach!